Real Estate Investing: Rental Properties and House Flipping

2-in-1 Books

No Need to Be a Millionaire to Become a Millionaire. Make Money in Real Estate and Live off Your Rents The Rest of Your Life

Earning Passive Income Through Rental Properties

Invest in Real Estate and Live off Your Rents. How to Do it With No Money and No Previous Knowledge in Rental Property and House Flipping

Table of Contents

Introduction 7
Chapter 1 - Understanding Rental Property Investment 11
  Why Rental Property? 11
  Two Ways to Earn Profits with Rental Property 14
  Developing the Right Mindset for Rental Property Success 17
Chapter 2—Great Location, Great Investment 22
  Classes of Real Estate, Where You Should Invest. 22
  Four Important Factors for Evaluating a Neighborhood. 24
  How to Spot an Emerging Real Estate Market. 26
Chapter 3—Choosing the Best Property 29
  Residential Real Estate to Invest In 29
  Types of Commercial Real Estate 31
  The 1% Rule for Investing in Real Estate 34
  Essential Questions to Keep in Mind When Evaluating Property 35
Chapter 4—Financing Your Rental Property 39
  House Hacking: Make Money and Live for Free 39
  Creative Ways to Finance Your Rental Properties 41
  Start Saving for a Down Payment Right Now 43
Chapter 5—Real Estate Tools for Success 49
  Strategies for Building a Successful Rental Property Portfolio. ... 49
  Commercial Real Estate, Another Means to Build Your Portfolio
  52

10 People You'll Need on Your Real Estate Dream Team 55

Chapter 6—The Rental to Outshine All Others 57

10 Steps for Rehabbing Your Rental Property 57

The Most Important Rehabs for All Rental Properties 61

Home Improvements to Instantly Boost the Value of Your Property 63

Chapter 7—Managing Your Rental 66

Finding Great Tenants for Your Rental 66

Strategies for Managing Rental Property 72

12 Must-Know Tips from Rental Property Experts 77

Chapter 8—Precautions 83

Good reasons to let go of rental property. 89

Five Crucial Exit Strategies for Your Real Estate Investments 91

Conclusion 94

Introduction

Does your uncle rent out his second apartment for $1500 a month and you want in on the action? Living the life of a landlord is a dream. Consider the possibilities: If you could rent 10 apartments for $1500 a month each, you could easily add $15,000 in passive income to your wallet every month for the rest of your life. Have you ever rented from a landlord who owns 5, 10 or maybe 50 condos, and makes a full-time living simply by renting properties? Do you ever wonder how they got there and got funding? In most cases, landlords didn't inherit their properties. They started out with a few acquisitions and expanded their ownership to numerous properties.

Do you want to get started in real estate but don't know where to find funding? There are ways to buy rental properties without being a millionaire. This book will teach you all the secrets you want to know about rental properties. If you have little or no money at all and don't know where to start, we'll teach you how to finance your rental properties without a significant investment. Yes, it's possible - and yes there are ways to secure hundreds of thousands of dollars without using your mom's house as collateral. We'll give you insight into the landlord mindset: You will learn how to finance properties with little to no initial investment and we'll tell you how to find tenants and enjoy a stress-free lifestyle for the rest of your life.

Revelation #1: Rental Properties Are Stable Income.

Renting is the easiest form of real estate investment, a lot easier than flipping properties full time. To become a landlord, you merely have to acquire a property and put it on the market. You'll be able to find tenants for even the worst, most run-down properties. Compare that to flipping, where the flipper has to put down a payment for a property, repair structural damage, refurbish the interior, and wait an average of six months while a house that might not sell at all sits on the market.

A landlord could technically purchase a property and rent it out the next day. So, you tell me which is easier, renting or flipping? The hard part of rental income is making a long-term profit. It's your job to learn how to finance multiple properties at once to be able to sustain mortgage payments from tenants and grow your portfolio. This allows you to create a mini real estate empire which you can use to lead a care-free lifestyle. However, getting there is the hard part. This book will teach you how to get your first rental properties.

Revelation #2: You Can Start With $0.

It's possible to start acquiring properties with $0 payment down or merely a few thousand dollars. Think you need to be a millionaire to become a landlord? Wrong! Rental income is far more risk-free than flipping income, as you could purchase the worst house and rent it out immediately – there's no need to repair the property. You don't have to spend money refurbishing the interior and you can get funding from private investors to purchase your rental property.

There are ways to convince financiers to finance your rental ventures in exchange for a monthly payment. Of course, the more money you have initially, the more money you'll get to keep in rental income at the end of each month. If you have a million dollars to spare, you could purchase multiple properties and start renting them out for serious income. If you have no money, you can reach out to private investors for funding or fund your properties via banking institutions. We'll show you the most viable methods to fund your rental properties for every budget.

Revelation #3: You Can Get Paid Every Week.

Rental Properties

Tenants will deposit payments in your bank account every week or every month. Technically, you could purchase a property and rent it on a daily basis to tourists on AirBnb, if you're willing to deal with clients every day. Rental property has no restrictions on the type of tenants you're allowed to have. The safest rental scheme is to provide housing for the average American family that has 2.5 children and a dog. However, that doesn't restrict your income.

If you have a property in a central location with many amenities, you could charge three times the market average to rent to tourists. Depending on how much time you're willing to spend dealing with tenants, you can adjust your payment terms accordingly. If you are willing to deal with tenants every day, you could get paid by the day. If you want a stable check deposited in your account at the end of each month, you can rent out to families. The latter is safer, but less profitable. The only work you'll have to do is bi-monthly checkups and annual maintenance (property taxes, insurance payments, etc.).

Revelation #4: There Is Work Involved.

We won't lie to you - rental income requires a certain amount of work. You won't have to call in general contractors and stress on the property every day like a flipper, but you will have to do to the occasional repair. What if you get a call at 3 a.m. from a tenant who has a roof leak? You can't tell them "go fix it yourself". You have to hire a roofing contractor who can get the job done and deal with that contractor for possibly weeks at a time. You're legally obliged to repair the property or you could face legal prosecution with fines and possible jail time. If a tenant dies as a result of property maintenance, the burden is on you.

Each time a problem arises in one of your properties, you will get a call from the tenants and they'll expect you to show up and fix it. It's your duty to hire the contractors and ensure that living conditions in your properties are up to par with the standards imposed by your state.

Like with any other business proposition, it's possible to skip the menial work. If you wish to disappear off the map, you could hire a "manager" do all the maintenance work for you and sail off into the sunset. However, most landlords live right next to their properties and assist tenants as problems arise due to trust issues. The most dedicated landlords in cities like New York own thousands of apartments and they attend to tenant's needs personally.

Revelation #5: Things Can Get Personal.

Have you ever rented your own apartment when you were a young adult and struggled to make payments? People run into financial distress all the time and your tenants won't be an exception. Certain landlords refuse to get close to their tenants and keep a business relationship in case they have to evict. Things can get ugly when you're dealing with tenants. Don't forget you're dealing with humans with real lives. The father renting from you might not be able to make rent after he's been fired from his job and the decision to evict him and his family will weigh on your conscience.

You'll have to make hard decisions. What if you're dealing with a single mother who has two babies to raise and she just lost her job and can't make rent? She may not realize that you still have to make your mortgage payments. Will you fall behind them or will you forgive their mortgage payment? You'll have to decide if you'll let them stay or if you'll evict them and make a place for new tenants. Landlord life is not glorious in many situations, despite how it's portrayed on TV shows. The more lower income your housing units are, the more you'll run into people with financial difficulties.

We'll give you the landlord secrets straight from the devil's mouth: We'll teach you how to finance properties, how to find tenants, and how to make a passive income with minimal work. Let's go!

Chapter 1 - Understanding Rental Property Investment

Why Rental Property?

Joe has $150,000 to invest. Why should Joe focus on rental properties instead of flipping properties? Rental is a whole different ball game. Rental properties are for the long term. For one, Joe can purchase a property he rents out without modifying the interior of the house. He can also start making a guaranteed profit as opposed to flipping a house that has to stay on the market for six months on average. Rental properties are for people who want long-term money, and who want to reap huge profits from depreciation. How many boomers do you know who bought a house for $100,000 in the 80's which is now worth over $1,000,000? If you hold on to your property for a decade or two, the value is guaranteed to double. In the meantime, you can get guaranteed monthly payments from tenants. We will teach you how to purchase properties, attract tenants, and get them to pay off your mortgages. For now, we'll show you why you need to invest in rental:

1) Real estate appreciation.

House prices in America go up. If you buy in a mid-sized city with population growth such as Austin, Texas, you're bound to see huge returns in as little as a few years. Appreciation means the property will increase in value the longer you hold on to it. People were able to purchase houses for a lot less than they cost today. The average $250,000 suburban house with a picket fence went for $100,000 in the 90s. What's not to say that the average $250,000 house of today will not be going for $500,000 within 15 years? The growth is bound to happen - you'll either buy in now or you'll miss out in the long run.

Rental Properties

Even if you ignore guaranteed monthly payments for each property, purchasing a property in a hot area means you'll make hundreds of thousands (if not even millions) over the long term. Remember, it's yours when you buy it (not the tenant's). You can sell and get rid of a property at any time.

The city and market have an effect on the appreciation. Historically, the wealthiest cities in the U.S., such as New York City and San Francisco, experience appreciation cycles and the average apartment in these cities can go for over $1M. However, you don't need to buy in Midtown Manhattan to get appreciation. You could buy in suburban Portland, Oregon and still see significant returns in 15 years. The best cities in which to invest are mid-sized cities with strong population growth. Do you know which cities have the highest growth per capita? They're not NYC or LA. They're mid-sized cities with booming economies such as Seattle, Atlanta, Austin, and Charlotte.

To be upfront, you will not make a significant amount of money within the first few years. You might not make any money at all within the first 5 years. However, you will double your investment within the first 10 years even if you invest in the most average neighborhood in the United States. Any decent area with good access to schools and convenience stores will do. You don't need exceptional and the property doesn't have to stand out. Go for a drive, and you'll notice almost all houses are average houses. Those houses increase in value as the U.S. economy produces more wealth. Get in on the action now or miss out.

2) Cash Payments from Tenants.

The tenant has to pay you by the month – you'll get a guaranteed $1000-2000 a month in profits for the average property. If you haven't figured it out, the average mortgage tends to be lower than $1000 while rents for a house are typically higher. This is where you'll make returns in the short term. If you don't have any money at all, you can make enough to cover a down payment on a mortgage and finance a $150,000 house. Once you become the owner, if your mortgage payment is $900 a month, you can rent the house for $1500 a month. This means your mortgage will be paid off and you'll have a few hundred left to spare. The tenant has to pay all bills unless and they're essentially paying off your mortgage. What's better than getting guaranteed payments without doing any work? You only have to pay the down payment, which is typically 20%. If that doesn't convince you to get into rental properties, nothing will.

If you have investment money to spare, you will keep all the profits without making mortgage payments. The $1500/month rent money will go directly in your pocket and you won't have to pay off the bankers – your only expenses will be the house insurance and yearly property tax, which is rarely above 2% of the total value of the property. Moreover, you have other rental avenues that are open to you. You could rent the property on a daily basis and charge a higher markup for holidays such as Christmas, New Year's, etc. This allows you to make two to three times the average profits of a rental property in your area. All properties rent out immediately, without any repairs necessary. House-flippers have to invest tens of thousands of dollars bringing a property up to current standards, while landlords only have to throw the property on the market.

3) Tax Rebates.

The IRS thinks rental properties are not the most profitable form of property and they have write-offs for virtually every type of property. Landlords can claim "losses" every year and get deductions for all their income taxes, which helps them keep more of their rental income. Rental investments are IRS-safe because the property appreciates and depreciates simultaneously. The IRS believes that properties depreciate due to tear and wear, however, the market is usually on the upswing and the property value for properties tends to increase.

Rental Properties

The IRS gives landlords write-offs under a specific property depreciation system called "General Depreciation System" or GDS. The GDS states that an average property has a recovery period of 27.5 years, which the IRS deems to be the average useful life of a property. The IRS provides deductions of precisely 3.6% per year on each building you own. In effect, the property taxes will be lower than the write-offs you're allowed. Using a simple write-off, you can pay the property tax and keep more of your profits using the GDS write-off.

4) Inflation Works In Your Favor.

Inflation raises the value of the property, while your mortgage payments remain the same. If you obtain a fixed-rate loan, which is the most popular of loans, you won't spend a single cent more than what you agreed to initially. For example, if you pay $20K as a down payment on a $100K property and that property appreciates to $200K within 10 years, you'll still only owe $80K. In effect, you only paid $20K to acquire a $200K property over 10 years. Inflation is your friend over the long-term and the fixed-priced mortgage allows you to only pay what you originally agreed to, instead of the inflated price of the property after you acquired it.

Two Ways to Earn Profits with Rental Property

1) Long Term Rentals

The safest and most conventional way to rent is long-term: You rent to families or professional individuals who have a job and the ability to make monthly payments. This is a foolproof rental method that requires monthly engagement with the tenant, only when you're collecting rent. You don't have to show up every week and check up on them and you only have to meet them when it's time to collect the rent. Long-term rent is the way to go, because families sign 6-month or 12-month contracts which are extendable.

Rental Properties

You can progressively increase the rent as properties in your area increase in value and the neighborhood becomes more desirable. For example, a house that rented out for $1000 this year might go for $1250 next year. Tenants don't like the rent increase? You'll find new ones in one week. The beauty of rental properties is that multiple people are competing for the property and you always have a viable pool of tenants to choose from, even in the most low-income areas. Here's how to calculate your bottom-line profits:

The 1% Rule of Long-Term Rentals

The 1% rule is the simplest calculation people use to estimate the profitability of a rental property. You can estimate the profitability of a rental property before you even purchase the actual property, which will give you an indicator as to how much bottom-line profits you'll have left with at the end of each month. The 1% rule states the following: If the GROSS monthly rent makes up 1% of the original purchase price, you should buy the property. If the monthly rent before expenses is less than 1% of the original purchase price, you should seek out other properties.

Let's say you find a house in decent shape for $100,000. How do you know if you'll make a profit renting it out? Simple: Use the 1% rule. The 1% rule states that your gross rent should exceed 1% of the original purchase price. The property has to rent out for at least $1000 a month if you want to make a Return on Investment (ROI). Under this rule-of-thumb, a $100,000 property has to rent out for $1000 a month and bring in 12% of the original purchase price in returns annually. In this particular example, the $100,000 property has to return $12,000 in annual gross profits before expenses such as property insurance, taxes, and bills. Your net revenue needs to be 6-8% of the total property value per year. This means that when you rent long-term, you should be making returns of $6000-8000 per year in pure profits on a $100,000 property.

Rental Properties

The average net return of 6-8% per year is a great deal, but it's going to depend on the city and neighborhood. The nicer the neighborhood, the lower the rental returns. The flipside is that a 6% return on a $300,000 house is higher than a 15% return on a $100,000 house. The highest rental returns typically found in cheap run-down properties exist because the properties cost little to purchase and the rental price is still relatively high. In general, you should be getting a solid 6% return in nice neighborhoods with affluent tenants and 8-10% returns on low-income neighborhoods with riskier properties that are more crime-prone. Whichever one you decide, you should not settle for less than 6% in yearly net returns.

The Capitalization Rate

Landlords calculate the "cap" rate, which is short for the capitalization rate, of the initial investment. The cap rate formula is the following:

Yearly Net Profits / Home Value = Cap Rate

Example: $8000 / $100,000 = 0.08

In this case, 0.08 is the result we're getting or 8% net ROI in simple terms. The capitalization rate on a $100,000 property which makes a net turnover of $8000 per year totals out to 8%. Whether 8% is a satisfactory return for the amount of effort you put into maintaining the property is up to you to decide.

The same principle applies to properties with a much higher property value. For example, if you find nice properties which give you an 8% cap rate on a $500,000 investment, you could make significant cash flow which pays off the property and gives you a great living. On the flip side, an 8% cap rate might not be worth it in a high-crime area that takes a lot to maintain and has extremely high insurance payments. In theory, you wouldn't need to be wealthy to finance a down payment on a $500,000 house, but you would have to save up for a few years.

2) Short-Term Rentals

Short-term rentals are the opposite of long-term rentals: They're unstable and they require constant work. You'll have to deal with clients a lot more than you would with long-term rentals, possibly daily. When you deal with long-term tenants, you only have to sign a contract and check them once or twice a month when it's time for you to collect your check or carry out the odd repair. With short term tenants, you have to meet tenants every day and clean up after them to prepare the property for the next tenants. What's in it for you? The markup is significantly higher. If you rent a house to a family for $1000 a month that wouldn't require any work on your end, but you'd only be left with $1000 at the end of each month. However, if you rent the same house for $100 a day to clients on AirBnb, you could make $3000 each month, but then you'd have to work and maintain the property every day.

Short-term rentals are the way to go if you have the time and patience to deal with clients on a daily basis. This is an excellent opportunity for young property owners or established property owners who enjoy meeting people and socializing. What's better than offering value to society and making huge returns in the process? You're not restricted to short-term rent from websites such as Craigslist and AirBnb. Once you own the property, you can convert it to a mini hotel or a hostel. It's possible to place four bunk beds in each room and convert the property to a hostel, then charge each one of the tenants $20 a night to stay there. This can generate a lot more cash flow than renting the property to a four-person family. Short-term rental requires a lot more work than long-term rental, but the profit margins are significantly higher.

Developing the Right Mindset for Rental Property Success

Rental Properties

The one thing all landlords agree with is that they're in it for the profit. However, individual motives for obtaining profit may be different. Some people become landlords to retire and live out the rest of their lives in peace. Some people become landlords to escape their 9-5 job and be able to survive without slaving at a dead-end job. Entrepreneurs who are motivated to become wealthy typically purchase multiple properties and rent them out while waiting for a high-ticket payout. Others become landlords by accident, by inheriting a few properties and converting them to rental units. We all have to deal with tenants, enforce payments and perform scheduled maintenance work. The property won't maintain itself and someone has to make the insurance and tax payments.

The landlord life is not a straight path, and we're driven into it for many reasons. If you want to retire, you will have to invest more in the property because the property has to be rentable over an extended period such as over multiple decades. For this purpose, you should purchase the newest and most expensive property possible. If you want to become wealthy and you don't plan to hold out to properties for too long, you can purchase semi run-down properties and make a higher markup renting them out. The following mindset tricks will be detrimental to your success in the rental property business:

1) The Cash Flow Mindset

The most essential landlord mindset is to develop an emergency cash-flow mindset. The faster you gather the cash to purchase the property or put down a deposit, the faster you'll be able to get out of your dead-end 9-5 job and/or retire. Remember you never have to cover the full purchase price of the property and you can get away with paying as little as 20%. If the rental home costs $100,000 you will only have to finance $20,000. How hard is it to save up this amount in today's economy? Even if you live in your mom's basement and work a minimum wage job, you should be able to save up $20,000 and put down a deposit on your first rental property. Don't be afraid to do the dirty jobs and the low-paid jobs because you'll only have to work them until you can finance your first property. Get two jobs! The faster you get the money, the faster you'll be able to finance your properties and create a new life for yourself.

Your focus should be on acquiring as many properties as possible and increasing the cash flow. If you're young and determined, you can afford to do short-term rentals and place an emphasis on increasing cash flow to milk the properties for the maximum amount of dollars viable. If you're reaching retirement age, you need to gather the investment funds you'll need to put down a deposit for stable properties that will pay for your retirement. The landlord mindset is not only about choosing properties and dealing with tenants, it's also about having a sense of urgency and gathering money for new properties. The faster you get at obtaining capital, the more money returns you'll see coming your way.

2) The Enforcer Mindset

The ugly truth about rental properties is that you'll have to deal with real human beings who might not be able to make rent - therefore you'll have to apply discipline and boundaries to make sure you're paid on time. This is especially critical during the first few months when you're getting established and missing a single payment could mean your property is one call away from being repossessed. You'll have to learn how to make your clients pay on time. In effect, you're becoming an enforcer that has to enforce the lease agreement.

What do you do when a tenant misses a payment? The tenant won't care that you have to make mortgage payments on the home; they'll only care for their individual situation. This is why the minute they fail to make a payment, you must file a late rent reminder. This reminder should go out in the first day they don't make a timely payment. The reminder has to have "grace period", which is the time they're allowed to go before they get an eviction warning.

If the tenant fails to pay in the grace period, you should file an eviction notice. The eviction notice notifies the tenant that civil court eviction action will be taken against them. The tenants will come to you with personal stories, but you shouldn't bend and give them leeway because they'll continue asking for more time. If you allow leeway once, they will know that your time is not important. If the landlord doesn't care, why should the tenants pay on time? Only give leeway when you don't have to make mortgage payments or it would compromise your personal relationship with a family member.

1) The Discipline Mindset

As a landlord you're not only supposed to perform monthly maintenance tasks where you greet your tenants, check up on the property, and collect rent. You must also carry out semi-annual and annual administrative tasks that require discipline and advance planning. What if you get hit with a $4000 bill on a roof leak? You'll need to prepare in advance. This takes discipline. Instead of spending your net profits on cruises in the Caribbean, set them aside for unexpected bills.

The lease terms should be drafted by a lawyer and have a paragraph mentioning a clause for semi-annual inspections which grant you the right to access the property. The properly won't need to have structural damage to warrant an inspection. The landlord shouldn't wait for things to go wrong before inspecting a property. Identify problems in advance and fix them! Make sure that your values are communicated clearly. If you don't tolerate smoking inside the property, you have to be prepared to evict a tenant if you detect smoke. Better yet, get a non-smoker tenant while you're signing the agreement.

Regular maintenance ensures that the property is well-mainlined and that your tenants don't experience problems inhabiting the property. The inspection is not only for property damage but unauthorized pets and people living on the property. While you're carrying out

Rental Properties

inspections, build up a personal relationship with your tenants. Feel free to ask them about their children, jobs, lives, etc.

Don't forget to raise the rent every year when the lease terms expire. Many landlords worry about raising rents. If you refuse to raise rents, your income will fall behind the market value and won't keep up with inflation. Raise the rents when the lease expires instead of raising it surprisingly at random times during the year, which scares tenants. This way you'll give them the option to pay higher rent prices or find a new property.

Chapter 2—Great Location, Great Investment

Now that we've given you a brief understanding of rental property investments, it's time to tell you about the different classes of real estate, what kinds of properties you can invest in, how you can evaluate target neighborhoods, and how you can identify emerging real estate markets that can generate large profits.

Classes of Real Estate, Where You Should Invest.

If you're going to get involved in the real estate market, you're going to need to familiarize yourself with the way different properties are classified or grouped. Although these classifications are somewhat subjective and there are no universal classifications or guidelines for how to identify properties, we can offer you some guidelines which should be helpful to you in grading specific locations or buildings. Real estate is often classified or graded similar to the way many of us were graded in high school or college, a letter grading system. These grading systems can go from A to C, A to D, A to F. A is obviously the highest rating; F is the poorest rating.

With real estate, the location often receives one rating and the building receives another rating. For example, if you have a great building in a mediocre area, you would have an A building in a C area. If you have an uninhabitable building in a questionable area, you would have an F building in a D area. Following are descriptions on how most people categorize locations with this grading system.

Rental Properties

An A location is in an area with the newest buildings, the hottest restaurants, and the best schools. You get the picture. It is an area that will have the highest rents.

An A building is a building that is most likely less than 10 years old. These buildings are likely to have the latest in granite countertops, hardwood floors, etc.

Rental properties in these A areas are likely to be high rent, low maintenance properties. They're easy investments, however it should also be noted that they may also bring a lower return on investment because of the higher demand and higher purchase price.

The B location is often in an area that has decent restaurants, albeit not the trendiest or most expensive restaurants. The schools are good, but not the brand new schools that some of the posh areas have. The area is home to mostly middle class, certainly more blue collar than the A areas. The people living in the B areas are much more likely to be living check to check.

The buildings in the B location are older, usually 15 to 30 years old. Most of these buildings have been upgraded, however not with the amenities of the A buildings.

As an investor in B properties, you'll find that they're likely to require more maintenance and attention than an A property would require. These properties will rent for less than A properties, but they are also capable of bringing you larger profits, because of the more moderate purchase price.

The C locations are marginal locations, often locations that are 30 years or older. The C buildings are often outdated and antiquated, in need of many and frequent repairs. C buildings often require plumbing and electrical upgrades; these buildings often require lots of attention and tender loving care. The upside of these C buildings is that they can often be purchased at a very moderate price; the downside is the amount of money you will likely have to spend to maintain or upgrade them.

D locations are dilapidated areas, often crime-infested and possibly dangerous. These are areas with many vacant or boarded up buildings. The buildings there are either neglected or uninhabitable. Unless you are a seasoned real estate investor, you'll probably want to stay away from investing in these areas. You would really have to know what you're doing to make money from a D building in a D area.

An F building and/or an F location can best be identified as a war zone. Crime-infested, drug-infested, struggling schools, homes and apartments in complete disrepair, etc. You get the picture; nothing that you should be interested in as a novice real estate investor.

Four Important Factors for Evaluating a Neighborhood.

Now that we've outlined the different classes of real estate, it's time to take a look at the different factors involved in evaluating the locations or areas in which you should invest. You've probably heard it before…there three major factors in real estate success: location, location, and location. Yes, that's an old cliché, but it still rings true. Location is almost always going to be the most important factor in the profitability of your real estate investments.

Most rental property investor newbies invest in properties which are near where they live. They do this because they are already familiar with the area, and also because properties in the near vicinity offer easy access for many of the responsibilities involved in rental property: showing the property, maintaining the property, rent collection, etc. Although owning rental property in the same area you live is most advantageous, there is a possible downside. If the economy in your area declines or tanks, you'll have all your eggs in one basket. If all your properties are in one area, they'll all be subject to the same

Rental Properties

factors which could affect the devaluation of the property, including a declining economy, increasing crime rates, weather disaster events (flooding, tornadoes and hurricanes, earthquakes), etc.

Here are some of the major factors for evaluating an area for possible rental property investment:

1) **Employment rate.** What's the employment rate in the area in which you are thinking of investing? That will have a major impact on how successful you can be with a rental property in that area. Obviously, if the unemployment rate in that area is high, you may find that it's an area in which it's going to be difficult to find and maintain reputable renters.

2) **Crime rate.** The crime rate in the area is also going to be a factor in whether you're going to be able to secure and keep renters. Major crimes such as homicides, sexual assaults, burglaries, robberies, and auto theft are certain to tarnish the reputation and livability of an area and those crimes and the reputation that follows them may impact your chance for success in that area or location.

3) **School system.** Does the area you're considering have a good school system? If you are going to be renting to families with kids, the school system in the area may impact your ability to rent a property. If the area has a good school system, you're likely to find that people will want to live in that area because of that. On the other hand, if the reputation of the area school system is lacking, you may find that people are looking to move out of the district.

4) **Vacancy/No Vacancy.** Is the area you're considering for rental property an area that has a lot of vacancies? Or are there barely any vacancies? This will also be an indicator of the possible success you might have in the area. If there are a lot of vacancies in your area,

commercial and residential, you're going to find it much more difficult to rent a property in that area. And you're likely to find that rental rates have much lower profit margins, as the market is much more competitive. If you drive through the neighborhood and find that many businesses or homes are boarded up or vacant, that's not a good sign. On the other hand, if you drive through the area and find that many residences or businesses are remodeling, that's a sign that people are investing in the area.

How to Spot an Emerging Real Estate Market.

If you're going to invest in rental properties, you're going to want to look for emerging real estate markets instead of submerging real estate markets. There are a number of sure indicators as to whether a market is flourishing or struggling. Although a lot of this information can be found online, you should not underestimate the value of finding out information on these areas by simply visiting the area and by meeting with the people who live and work in the area. Although data and analytics are important in making real estate decisions, you should never disregard the "eye test" as part of your decision making.

One determinant to consider in your real estate investments is the population growth of the area. Is the area growing, is it stable or stagnant, is it declining? Obviously, population growth and the corresponding demand for housing is desirable for real estate investors. You'll likely want to tie yourself to an area that is growing in selecting the areas in which you own real estate.

Another factor to consider is existing home sales. Even if an area appears to be economically depressed, an increase in existing home sales can be a strong indicator that an area is reemerging or coming back. As a real estate investor, you need to be aware that areas and neighborhoods often regenerate themselves and if you can get into

Rental Properties

these areas early in the process, you'll stand to make a lot more profit than you would if you are a latecomer. That being said, some areas and neighborhoods never regenerate and it will be important for you to identify these areas as you decide whether or not to invest in them. Existing home sales within the area are a key indicator to the possible vitality of the area. When reviewing statistics for any area, it is important to note that you'll need to fine tune these statistics as much as possible. For example, if you are looking at making a real estate investment in the Atlanta area, it's important for you to refine that information to a smaller area. Atlanta is a large metropolitan area and there are neighborhoods within that area that are flourishing and other neighborhoods that are struggling at any given time. So, you will need to certainly refine your information search down to a zip code or preferably even a neighborhood within a zip code.

Rising rental rates are another strong indicator in spotting an emerging real estate market. If rental rates are increasing steadily year after year, this is an indication that the real estate market within the area is healthy and a possible target for investment. If you're interested in determining rental rates in a given area, Zillow's rent index provides valuable information, including the median estimated market rate rent across any specific region and housing type.

Also, new construction within an area is an indicator that the area is healthy from a real estate standpoint. The Residential Construction Index provided by the U.S. Census Bureau contains valuable information about the number of building permits which are issued for a particular area and also the number of new homes which are started and completed each month.

Foreclosure rates within any given area are another indicator of real estate investment potential. As someone interested in rental property, you'll probably want to steer clear of areas that have increasing foreclosure rates.

Rental Properties

Also, there are less conventional factors which might indicate whether an area is a good target for investment. Has a large company announced that it is relocating to the area or that it is opening a branch in the area? If so, it follows that the employees at this new location will be relocating also. Some of them will be looking to move closer to their workplace. Either way, that can only be good for the economy of the area. On the downside, has a large employer announced that they will be leaving the area? If so, this move is likely to have a negative impact on the local economy.

Another less conventional indicator of real estate rental potential is to determine the normal amount of time it takes for a house to be sold or rented. If that average time frame is over six months, that may well be an indicator that the market is flat and not a good candidate for current investment. On the other hand, if those homes are selling or renting in 30 days, that is a very good sign and it's an indicator that the area is a good investment target.

Chapter 3—Choosing the Best Property

Now that you know more about how to evaluate properties and areas and how to identify areas that are good investment targets, it's time to talk about how to choose the types of real estate investments which will work best for you. This is an important part of the process, as some retail estate investor wannabes make the mistake of choosing an area of real rental that does not fit their interests or their personality.

Residential Real Estate to Invest In

You may be surprised to learn that there are many different types of real estate to invest in, including a number of different types of residential real estate:

1) **Single family homes.** These are the most popular type of rental homes. Although single family homes also include some of the other types of homes listed below (apartment, condos, townhomes, coops, luxury homes, vacation homes), single family homes are the largest category of residential real estate.

2) **Condominiums/coops.** Although condos and coops are single family homes, they are a bit different in that they are managed by a homeowner's association. The homeowner's association is often responsible for the common areas and responsibilities for the complex, including garbage collection, landscaping, common area maintenance, and often exterior maintenance of the individual units. In return, the homeowner's association collects a fee from all members. If you are going to rent out a unit that is managed by a homeowner's association, you'll have to incorporate the homeowner's fees into the rent amount you charge your tenants.

3) **Multi-family homes.** Multi-family units are properties that include two or more dwellings which are rented out separately. This includes apartment building, duplexes, and triplexes. With some real estate investors, the owner is living in one of the units and is then renting out the other units. Owning multi-family homes is slightly more complicated than owning single family homes, as the performance of the property is based on the performance of each unit individually. Also, you should know that multi-family homes are sometimes classified as commercial properties, depending on the number of units involved.

4) **Luxury homes.** Luxury homes are top-quality homes which contain the latest amenities, technologies, and appliances. These are properties that demand top-dollar rental rates. And they are the most expensive homes to invest in.

5) **Vacation homes.** Vacation homes are often rented out on a seasonal basis, with the rental rates fluctuating from high during the peak season to lower during non-peak season. Most vacation homes are located in tourist areas. Areas in Texas, Florida, and Arizona have plenty of vacation homes to accommodate "snowbirds", people from northern areas of the U.S. trying to escape the cold weather and snow of the winters. Investors also own vacation homes along the coasts in various locations. Others own vacation homes near tourist destinations such as Disney World. And lake homes in the northern areas of the country such as Minnesota, Michigan, and Wisconsin, can also be good investments. One of the advantages of owning a vacation property is that the owners will often use these properties for their own vacations or getaways and then rent out the property for the remainder of the year.

Types of Commercial Real Estate

Commercial real estate covers a lot of different types of real estate, all the way from single office buildings or spaces to massive skyscrapers, airports, stadiums, amusement parks, and shopping malls. As a real estate rental newbie, we're going to presume that you're closer to the lower end of investors, but you should know that almost all of the types of commercial real estate we're listing include both small and large properties. Because of the costs involved, commercial real estate is almost always a higher stakes game. By the same token, most commercial leases are longer than residential leases, because of the accommodations which are normally made to the building or the property for the tenants.

1) **Office space.** This is the most common commercial property. The office space spectrum ranges from single tenant properties to skyscrapers and office complexes which are home to hundreds of tenants and thousands of their employees. Like residential properties, commercial properties are classified on grade levels (i.e.—A, B, C). Class A commercial real estate consists of new buildings or recently refurbished/extensively refurbished buildings. They are normally in excellent areas and normally managed by professional management companies. Class B commercial real estate is the most popular class for investors. Class B properties are generally slightly older buildings that require some capital investment for minor repairs or upgrades. Class C commercial properties are often old buildings that are targeted for major renovations or redevelopment. Those who invest in Class C properties can generally expect major capital investments to bring the property up-to-date and to make it marketable to tenants. Vacancy rates are usually much higher for Class C properties and these properties are much more difficult to lease.

2) **Retail.** Again, the spectrum range is huge, ranging from a print shop that might have two or three employees to a restaurant or bank that might have 50 employees to a huge shopping mall that might have thousands of employees. Retail properties are often located in urban areas or business districts. Most shopping malls are owned by large investment groups, but on the lower end of the spectrum, some of the smaller retail locations are owned by single, mom-and-pop, or family investors.

3) Industrial. Industrial properties range from manufacturing facilities to warehouse facilities. They often require larger amounts of space to accommodate dock areas for shipments that come in and go out. These industrial properties are generally in lower rent, lower traffic areas, as they are lower profile businesses that do not require prime real estate.

4) Multi-family. This includes residential locations that have as few as four units. It also includes large apartment complexes and high-rise condominium complexes. Many residential property investors who want to get into commercial real estate choose to get into commercial real estate by investing in multi-family properties such as apartment buildings that can accommodate anywhere from four to a dozen tenants. As we discuss commercial real estate in this chapter, it should be pointed out that residential leases are often much shorter than commercial leases. Most residential leases have six or 12-month terms. Most commercial leases will range from three to 20 years, depending on the building and the business. Commercial leases are normally longer because the owner often has to make accommodations to the building in order to fit the tenant's business. And then when that tenant leaves, the building or space generally has to be repurposed or remodeled to fit the next tenant.

5) Special purpose. As long as we just mentioned repurposing, we should also mention special purpose commercial real estate. This is generally a building that is built for a unique or special purpose and can not often be repurposed without a lot of renovation. Businesses such as car washes, schools, and storage facilities are considered special purpose locations. For example, if you own a property and are leasing to a tenant who has a car wash, it's not going to be easy to repurpose that building if and when the tenant leaves. You're either going to have to lease to another tenant who wants to use the facility as a car wash or you're going to have to be prepared to make major accommodations or renovations for the next tenant. That's why leases for special purpose buildings are generally much longer than leases for other types of commercial real estate.

And while we're discussing special purpose commercial real estate, we should also mention mixed use developments. These developments have become extremely popular in recent years, mostly in urban areas. An example of a mixed use development would be a multiple story apartment complex with a business or businesses on the ground floor. That business might be a pizza restaurant, a health club, or even a supermarket. Generally, the business located on the ground floor of the complex is a retail location which can benefit financially from the tenants above. Along the same lines, large corporations have mixed use buildings in which their offices constitute a large amount of the space, but then they lease the remaining space to other retail businesses who can benefit from the large number of employees. As an example, a large corporation in the electronics industry has a campus with multiple buildings and thousands of employees. They allow certain retail companies to rent space within their building, including coffee companies, a dry cleaners, a health club, and a doctor's office. The feeling is that not only can these businesses benefit from the corporation's large numbers of employees, the corporation is also making things more convenient for employees who no longer need to leave the premises for some of their errands or activities.

6) **Owner occupied.** Some real estate investors purchase property with the intent of using it for their own purposes. And some of these investors will use a portion of the space for themselves and then rent out other portions to tenants. This strategy can be applied to many of the commercial real estate options discussed above.

The 1% Rule for Investing in Real Estate

We previously mentioned the 1% Rule. As you consider which real estate investments to make, you'll need to use some kind of measurement tool to determine how much rent you would need to charge for a property, commercial or residential. You'll need to make sure that the rent you are charging your tenants will at least cover all of your expenses for the property; hopefully more, so you can make a profit. After all, most of us do not intend to get into the real estate business as a hobby; most of us are looking to make a profit. The 1% rule for investing is one way you can determine how much rent you'll need to charge for any rental property you invest in. Here's how it works. (Excuse us for being a bit redundant, but it's absolutely imperative that you have a measurement tool for the amount of rent you'll need to charge to derive income from the property.)

With the 1% rule, you simply multiply the purchase price of the property by 1% to determine the base level of the monthly rent you will need to charge. For example, if you purchase a property for $300,000, you'll multiply that by 1% to get a base rate of $3000. That $3000 will be the base you should work from in determining a rent level from a tenant. But please know that this is just the base level and you will also need to consider other expenses for the property, including things such as insurance, taxes, and upkeep. Upkeep can include things such as garbage collection, janitorial services, snow removal, and landscaping. Those expenses will also need to be accounted for as you work to determine your rent level and your break-even point.

Obviously, the rent or rents you are charging need to cover your mortgage payments (unless you are indeed investing in real estate as a charity or a hobby.) If the property you are interested in will require any major repairs or renovations before it can be leased, you'll need to add those cost estimates to the purchase price before you calculate the 1%. For example, if the $300,000 property you're interested in will require a $20,000 roof repair before it is marketable, you'll add that $20,000 before you divide by 1%. As an investor, you should ideally seek a mortgage loan with monthly payments that are less than the 1% figure you've calculated.

Again, there are many other factors to consider in evaluating the profit potential of a property, but the 1% rule at least gives you a base to work from in determining what rent level you would need to charge and what kind of mortgage payments you should look for in purchasing the property.

Essential Questions to Keep in Mind When Evaluating Property

Investing in real estate for rental is a major consideration and you'll need to make sure you ask yourself the correct questions in evaluating any property. Here are some questions you should be asking as you consider purchasing rental properties:

1) **Will the location make for a solid investment?** As mentioned before, location might be the major factor in whether a rental property is profitable. In evaluating any location, there are a number of things to consider. Is the location near to amenities that your prospective tenants are going to require? If you're planning to rent to young families with kids, nearby amenities such as good

schools, supermarkets, gyms, and restaurants will enhance your investment. If you are planning to rent to senior citizens, nearby amenities such as supermarkets, doctors' offices and medical clinics, and health clubs will be attractive to prospective renters. If you are thinking of renting to college students, nearby bars, restaurants, and gyms may enhance the attractiveness of your property. Another thing to consider with location is whether the area contains a large enough pool of prospective renters. For example, if you have an upscale property in an area where mostly middle class workers reside, you may have difficulty renting that property. If you have a low-rent Class C property in an area that is predominantly upscale residents, you may have difficulty renting. So, make sure that your location matches the pool of prospective renters you're targeting. If you can make sure your pool of prospective tenants matches your property, you'll ensure that you have consistent rental income over the time you own the property.

2) Is the property functional? If not, what's it going to take to make it functional? It's okay to buy a property that needs repairs, even major repairs. However, before you purchase such a property, you'll have to determine how much it's going to cost and how long it's going to take to make the property functional. Novice investors are notorious for underestimating the costs involved in fixing up a property. We've heard some people say that if you are estimating costs and time frame for a property you should simply take whatever figures you come up with and double them. They live by the mantra, "If something can go wrong, it's likely to go wrong." So, if they have calculated renovation costs of $20,000, they'll be thinking that they could end up spending up to $40,000 for the renovation. If they calculate six weeks to do the renovation, they'll be aware that they renovation could take up to three months if things don't go as planned.

In evaluating the property you're interested in, you will have to determine what items you can fix yourself and what items you'll have to hire contractors for. And then you'll have to secure quotes for the work from those contractors. And obviously, you'll also have to price out materials costs for any renovation. This can be a somewhat complicated process; that's why many novice rental real estate investors will opt to purchase properties which do not require major renovations. They'll take the attitude that at least they have a better indication of what they are getting into as far as costs are concerned. If you're not experienced in renovating properties, you're more likely to stumble upon some expensive surprises in fixing up a property.

Also, you should know that when we are referring to a functional property, we are also referring to a property that is easily rentable to tenants and one that is safe for tenants. If these things aren't happening, you'll limit your ability to rent the property or you may endanger a tenant to the point where you are risking their safety or risking a serious insurance claim against you. For example, if you have a leaky roof, that will almost surely impact your ability to rent the property or, even, if you rent it, may jeopardize your ability to keep renting the property. Or, if your roof is in total disrepair, you might actually endanger the safety of a tenant.

3) **What's it going to cost to maintain the property?** In evaluating the viability or possible profitability of a rental property, you'll also need to determine what it is going to cost to maintain it. For example, if you own a small office complex, you're probably going to have to pay for landscaping and garbage collection. If you have common areas in the building, you'll have to pay for janitorial services, including restroom maintenance. If you're in a northern area, you'll probably have to pay for snow plowing or removal. All of these maintenance costs will have an impact on the profitability of your rental property. And you should note that there may be more costs involved in some rentals than in others. For example, if you are renting out a vacation property that turns over tenants frequently, you'll have to pay more to frequently prepare the property for new tenants. If you are renting a property to college students who may use it as a party

Rental Properties

house, you may have to pay higher damage or repair costs as you prepare for new tenants. Is the property close to where you are living or working? Will you be willing to make any minor repairs yourself or will you need to hire a management company to handle these repairs? Those are all things to think about when you are evaluating the viability of a rental property.

Besides repair and routine maintenance costs, you'll have to ask yourself some other questions regarding the viability of the property. What are the expected property taxes? Projected insurance costs? What are the vacancy rates for the area the property is located in? How will you accommodate vacancy expenses? Will you have a separate fund set up for that or will you have to borrow money for that? (Hopefully, not the latter.) Is the rent amount you'll have to charge for the property competitive with rates being charged for similar properties in the same area? Is the property locating in a flourishing area? Declining area? Are there any changes coming to the area that will impact the economy? (i.e.—A major company coming to the area or leaving the area? Light rail or other major transportation routes coming to the area? A sports stadium coming to the area? This might impact parking availability in the area and make a residential property less desirable. On the other hand, it might also offer more opportunities in regards to commercial real estate for new restaurants, bars, and hotels.

Buying an investment property can be complicated. The upside is that rental property can also be very profitable. But you'll want to make sure that you've asked yourself all the necessary questions before you invest in any property. Miscalculating any of these factors could well make the difference between being profitable or losing money on your investment.

Chapter 4—Financing Your Rental Property

We've been talking about why owning rental property is a good idea, the different types of rental property investments to consider, and things to consider in choosing a rental property. Now it's time to tell you about the ways you can finance a rental property. There are multiple ways to do this, including some ways for first-time investors to enter the market.

House Hacking: Make Money and Live for Free

Some of you may not be familiar with the term "house hacking", so before we get into how to do it, we should explain what it is. House hacking involves the renting or leasing of owner-occupied properties to tenants in an effort to subsidize the occupany costs for the owner. House hacking is particularly popular with young, single investors. Here's how it works. A person will purchase a home (or office location) with the intention to live in that home. They'll then rent that home out to one or more occupants and use that rental income to subsidize or finance the cost of the property. As an example, a recent college grad opts to buy a starter home and then share it with two roommates. His mortgage payment is $1100 a month and he charges each of his roommates $600 a month in rent to cover the cost of his mortgage and some of the additional costs of the house, including water and electric. In essence, the recent college grad is able to live in the home for free, and at the same time, have his tenants pay for the equity he accumulates in the home.

The upside for the roommates is that they pay less to live in his home than they would to rent a one bedroom apartment. At the same time, they have more space and possibly more amenities than they would get with a one bedroom apartment.

The possible downside to the owner is that he has share his living quarters and he may prefer more privacy. (On the other hand, he may enjoy the company.) As most of us who have shared a living area know, the living arrangement will work much better if the parties are compatible. Also, there may be some security risks if you rent to a stranger. We've heard the story of a man who shared his home with a roommate, only to come home one day to find that all of his major belongings had disappeared.

It should also be pointed out that house hacking doesn't always involve roommates. It's not uncommon for some house hackers to purchase duplexes or triplexes, living in one of the units and then renting out the other units to others. This affords the owner a lot more privacy than he would receive in sharing a unit with roommates.

Let's outline the benefits of house hacking:

1) **You can decrease or eliminate your housing expense.** As you all know, for most of us, our housing expensive is usually our largest monthly expense. Statistics show that Americans spend about 40% of their income on housing. In house hacking, you will be able to substantially reduce or eliminate those expenses. And for the recent college grads who are living with parents, house hacking also offers more independence than you'll have cohabiting with your parents.

2) **Increase your income, savings.** Many people look at the house hacking stage as a transitional stage or temporary stage which allows them to work toward their own financial independence while they pay off school or car loans or save money toward the next home after the starter home. Some people will house hack as they work toward a second investment property; others will simply use the money to pay for a nice vacation.

3) Get some experience as a landlord. Living with tenants will allow you to get your feet wet in the world of being a landlord. In listening to the wants, needs, and concerns of your tenants, you'll get an inkling of what it's like to be a landlord. You'll also get an inkling of the things that can go wrong for a landlord (roof leaks, tenant late on the rent, refrigerator stops working, etc.). When repairs are required, you'll learn to solve problems, either by repairing the items yourself or enlisting someone to do the repairs for you.

4) Owning property. In owning property as a house hacker, you'll be establishing equity on the property. At the same time, your investment value may be escalating and when you go to sell the property, you'll reap the benefits of the escalated value.

Creative Ways to Finance Your Rental Properties

The conventional way to purchase a rental property is to save up for the down payment and then secure a mortgage to cover the remaining amount. There are however some other ways you can finance the purchase of a rental property.

1) House Hacking. As outlined above, house hacking is a popular way to finance your first rental property.

2) Seller Financing. Some sellers are willing to loan money for the purchase of their property. Some of them are willing to loan the entire amount of the purchase; others are willing to loan the down payment amount. If you can do this, you might find that it is a much simpler process than a bank loan with less paperwork. As someone who is buying the property, you'll want to make sure that you are getting a fair interest rate for the purchase. Unless you're very experienced in purchasing real estate properties, you will be well advised to consult with an attorney and/or CPA in initiating this purchase. And whatever you do, make sure you get your agreement in writing. For many of you, this will be one of the largest purchases of your life and you will certainly want to make sure that it is properly documented.

In discussing seller financing, you should know that many sellers do not advertise that they offer financing. If you are truly interested in seller financing as an option, you should ask the seller if they are willing to offer financing. It's possible that the seller hasn't thought about this before and you may find that they are so interested to sell the property that they will be willing to offer you financing at a good rate.

3) **Partnerships.** If you don't have enough money for a down payment, you might secure a partner in your purchase. Do you have a friend or family member who would be willing to partner with you in purchasing a rental property? Although you can structure a partnership agreement any way you want, you should know that with a lot of real estate partnership agreements, one partner will make the down payment and then the other partner will handle all of the landlord duties, including collecting rent, making or arranging repairs, corresponding with tenants, etc. In essence, the person making the down payment is generally a silent partner. In return for the down payment, the two partners then agree to split the profits derived from the rental income and also when the property is sold. Again, these partnership agreements can be structured any way you and your partner want, but the basic tenet of the partnership is that one partner will provide the funds while the other will do the work.

Many partnerships are limited liability companies (LLCs) in which you can specifically outline your agreement and the corresponding roles and responsibilities of each party. LLCs are great in that they will also allow you to protect your personal assets in the event your business or partnership is ever sued. As we recommend previously in regards to seller financing, all partnership agreements should be outlined in writing. Verbal agreements and handshake agreements are not advised for such a major purchase. If you don't have a relationship with an attorney who can initiate an LLC or partnership agreement for you, companies such as Rocket Lawyer or LegalZoom are available online to help you draft simple legal agreements.

4) **Government programs.** You may or may not be familiar with FHA, the Federal Housing Administration. The FHA offers reasonable loans for owner-occupied properties, including single homes, duplexes, triplexes, and quadruplexes or four-unit apartment buildings. The loan rate for FHA loans is very reasonable at 3-1/2%. Loan limits for FHA loans are different in every county, so, if you're interested in FHA financing, we suggest that you find out what the loan limit is in your county before you get too far along in your search for rental investment properties.

5) **Retirement accounts.** If you're a bit older and you have some retirement accounts you can draw from, this is another good way to finance the purchase of a rental property. If you have a self-directed IRA (Individual Retirement Account), you're not restricted to traditional assets such as stocks or mutual funds. You're also allowed to invest those funds in non-traditional assets, including rental property. Again, we're going to suggest that you consult with a professional in using retirement accounts funds for a real estate purchase, whether that is a financial planner or a certified public accountant. Purchasing a rental property is serious business and you should not try to do so without professional counsel, unless you are experienced at doing so.

Start Saving for a Down Payment Right Now

Rental Properties

As someone who is already this far into the book, it seems as if you have a sincere interest in purchasing and owning a rental property. That being said, you may be asking yourself how in the world you're ever going to accumulate the amount you'll need to actually purchase that property. In this chapter, we've outlined some simple thoughts on how you can save enough money to make a down payment. Most of these ideas are financial planning techniques that can be successful for anyone who is looking to save enough money for any particular purchase.

1)   The Percentage Plan. In using the percentage plan, we encourage you first to determine where all of your income is normally being spent. We suggest that you detail all of your mandatory or fixed expenditures within the past 90 days. Mandatory or fixed expenditures will be payments you have to make and will include things such as rent, utilities, school and car loans, food, gas, cable television, internet services, cell phone, etc. These payments should be easy to track, as you'll have receipts for most of them. Although some of these payments will vary slightly from month to month (i.e.—Your electric bill might be $60 one month and $70 another month), you should have enough information to figure out what your average monthly expenditure is. You'll then place all of these mandatory or fixed expenses in one category and move to the next category, which we'll call discretionary spending.

Discretionary spending covers remaining expenses that aren't necessary expenditures—things such as health club or gym memberships, the daily cup of joe you get from your neighborhood coffee shop, bar/restaurant/entertainment expenses, weekend getaways and vacations, etc. After you've listed all of the discretionary expenditures you can remember, you should then review these expenditures and see if any of them could be eliminated without severely cramping your lifestyle. Are you using your gym membership? Can you do without the daily cup of coffee from the

Rental Properties

neighborhood coffee shop? Do you really need to eat at restaurants three times a week? Can you do without a weekend getaway? Do you really need the premium cable tv package or could you make do with the less expensive basic package? In listing all of your discretionary expenses for the past 90 days, you'll be able to see how you are spending your money. If you can eliminate or reduce any of your discretionary expenditures, you should then be able to allocate these funds toward saving for a rental property down payment.

After you've totaled your fixed expenditures and determined what your discretionary expenditures should be, you should calculate what portion of your income each of these two categories accounts for. Most people find that fixed expenditures account for anywhere from 50 to 70 percent of their income. Your fixed expenditures are mostly non-negotiable. Maybe you can cut a small amount off your cable tv package by dropping some of the premium channels. Maybe you can carpool or consolidate your errands to save on gas expenditures. But for the most part, your fixed expenditures are what they are.

Your discretionary expenditures are exactly as described…they're discretionary. You should determine exactly which of these expenditures you can't do without and which of those you could either eliminate or reduce. After you've determined the amount you want to allocate on a monthly basis for discretionary activities, you should then see what percentage of your income these expenditures entail. And then see how much is left over for savings.

Some people will end up with a 70/20/10 plan. (70% fixed, 20% discretionary, 10% savings.) Others will end up with a 50/30/20 plan. You'll go with whatever works best for you, however the important thing is the savings category, as you'll use those funds to make the down payment on your rental property.

In setting a monthly limit for you discretionary spending, you will be able to save an accumulate the funds necessary to purchase your rental property. Are you an impulse spender? If so, you're the type of person who is likely to have the most difficulty in controlling your discretionary spending. If this is the case and you need help in controlling your monthly expenditures, there are apps that can help you do so. *Mint* is a popular app which can help you with your discretionary spending by alerting you when you are nearing the monthly limit you've assigned to your discretionary spending. When you get a "warning" that you're near your limit, maybe that warning will help you dial back your Amazon purchases or your Starbuck's coffee purchases.

Again, there's no set rule on how to set up your own income percentage plan. Whatever works for you should be fine, as long as you're setting aside a monthly amount you'll need for the down payment on your rental property.

2) **Reverse Engineer.** Another way you can determine how long it's going to take you to save for your rental property down payment is to work backwards using reverse engineering. In doing so, you'll first determine the approximate price of the property you'll be looking to buy. For purposes of this example, we'll use $100,000 as the number to work with. We realize that this number may be extremely low for certain areas of the country, but it is an easy number to work with, especially for the mathematically impaired. Ha.

So, if, for example, you're thinking of purchasing a $100,000 property, you'll know that you'll have a 20% down payment on that property ($20,000). In addition to the down payment, you'll have closing costs that normally range from 1-2% of the down payment. You'll also need a contingency fund of maybe another 1-2%. For purposes of this example, let's keep it simple and list both the closing costs and the contingency/rainy day fund at $2000 each. So, coupled with the $20,000 down payment, you will need approximately $24,000 to purchase a $100,000 property. If you want to purchase the rental property in two years, you'll then divide the $24,000 total amount by

24 months. This will show you that you will need to save $1000 a month to reach your two-year savings goal. If this is too ambitious, you can always change your savings plan from 24 to 30 or 36 months. Or you can make the decision to look for less expensive/lower-priced properties. Again, there is no set prescription for how to establish a savings plan. You'll have to decide what works best for you or what you can live with. The goal of these savings plans is simply to get you to do the math in determining what it will take to accumulate the funds to purchase a rental property and then to put a plan into action.

3) Automate Your Budget. It's no secret that lack of will power is the most common deterrent to any budget. You resolve to control your spending at the beginning of the month and then a few days into the month you find the signed National Football League jersey you've been looking for on ebay or the designer bag you've been looking for on Amazon. So much for the budget you set up at the start of the month. Five days in and you've already blown your discretionary budget limit. If this is you and if you have difficulty controlling impulse purchases, you might consider automating your payments, especially your savings payments.

If, after reviewing your expenditures, you've determined that you can save $750 a month, go ahead a set up an automatic payment once or twice a month from your checking account to a separate savings account you've designated for your rental property purchase. You should have a good idea as to when you get paid and you'll know whether you get paid monthly or semi-monthly. Set up the automated deposits to your savings account soon after your paychecks are deposited. Maybe a day or two after. At the same time, set up all of your other fixed expenditures to be paid automatically at the same time, possibly on the same days. Then whatever funds are left in your account that month, you'll be able to use as you see fit for your discretionary purchases. In setting up automated payments, you'll make sure that all of your fixed expenses are paid. You'll also be

Rental Properties

safeguarding the amounts you want going into savings, as those amounts will be deposited before you make any discretionary purchases.

As mentioned earlier in this chapter, we suggest that you review all of your expenditures before you set up any budget plan and then determine if there are any areas which you can eliminate or reduce expenditures. Cut out the things which are not adding value to your life.

Chapter 5—Real Estate Tools for Success

Now that you know how to accumulate the funds you'll need to make the down payment on your first rental property, let's expand the picture and talk about some ways you can build a real estate portfolio and the people you'll want to have on your real estate "team" if you have multiple properties.

Strategies for Building a Successful Rental Property Portfolio.

One of the main reasons the real estate rental market is so attractive is because home ownership is dwindling and the percentage of people who are renting is increasing. That's been happening for a couple of decades now, and with the price of homes continuing to rise, that trend probably won't change any time soon. With this in mind, it's a great time to invest in real estate rental properties and establish a portfolio of profitable properties that will leave you financially set for the rest of your life. Here are a number of different ways you can establish your real estate portfolio past your first rental property:

1)   Buy Multi-Family Units. We've detailed many of the benefits of multi-family units previously in this book. If you want to build your real estate "empire", one of the best ways to do that is to start purchasing multi-family units. Real estate investment newbies often start with owner-occupied multi-family units such as duplexes, triplexes, and quadruplexes; they then graduate to larger multi-family units such as apartment complexes. In owning multiple units at the same location, you'll be able to consolidate your efforts and costs. An owner who has four single family rental homes will obviously have to put in a lot more time, effort, and running around than an owner who owns a quadruplex. So, if you want to start expanding your real estate rental empire, multi-family properties are a great place to start.

2)   The Snowball Method. Warren Buffet is one of the most successful investors of all time and he has had a lot of success using the snowball method of investing. Most of us who live in the northern areas of the US are familiar with how to build a snowball; some of you in the South may never have experienced snow. So, I'll remind you how a snowball is made. You start with a small ball of snow that often fits in your hand. As you roll that snowball along the snow-covered ground, it gathers additional snow and the ball gets bigger and bigger. We've seen instances of people who make snowballs taller than they are.

The same goes with the snowball method of investing. Instead of using the profits from your first rental property to buy new vehicles or to take luxurious vacations, you can use that profit toward the purchase of another property. Many investors use this philosophy (and some of them don't even know it). It's a great way to expand a real estate empire and, if your properties are profitable, you'll surely find that you'll pick up momentum as you go along. And you'll have a much wider selection of properties to choose to invest in as you make more money. You'll be able to graduate from one single family home or a duplex into multiple single family homes or multi-unit properties, including apartment complexes. So, you'll be wise to let the money you make from your rental property investments work for you. Instead of using those profits solely for personal amenities, you'll be wise to use those funds in other investments.

3)   Start with Partnerships. We discussed some of the benefits of partnerships in the section on how to secure the money to buy your first rental property. Partnerships can also work well beyond the first property. As you get more heavily into real estate investment, you may want to "up the ante" on the properties you're investing in.

Rental Properties

You're likely to want to invest in larger, more expensive units. Having an investment partner will allow you to do this more quickly and it will also reduce your financial exposure on the property you're investing in. Also, as far as financing goes, you may find that the banks that financed your previous mortgages, may eventually be reluctant to provide additional mortgages because they don't want to "have all of their eggs in one basket".

4) **The C-B-A Strategy.** We previously discussed the different classes of real estate. Class A properties are generally the premier properties—new buildings in great areas. Repairs generally not necessary. Class B properties are generally slightly older properties in good areas. Maybe minor repairs necessary. Class C properties are often marginal properties in marginal areas with many minor or even some major repairs required. Many real estate investors who are trying to build a portfolio will start by investing in Class C properties and then work their way up to Class B and then Class A properties. The C properties are less expensive than A properties and they require a lot more work initially. In starting out with C or B properties, you'll quickly get a good education on what it takes to be a successful rental property investor. Then as you accumulate money from these Class C properties, you'll be able to invest in the more expensive Class B or Class A properties. As we say this, you should know that some investors choose to stay mostly in the same class. We know successful investors who stay mostly with Class B properties instead of ever moving to Class A properties because they find the B properties to be more profitable or more plentiful…or they just feel more comfortable in that area. Either way, you get the idea…you have to learn to take baby steps first before you can walk, and you have to learn to walk before you can run.

5) **Mix It Up.** One of the keys to having a successful real estate portfolio is to mix it up…have a diversified portfolio. Some investors get stuck in staying with properties that work for them. Maybe they

buy only residential properties and no commercial properties. Maybe they buy only Class B properties. Maybe they buy only properties in the same area of town. Although there is certainly something to be said about staying with what works for you, the "if it ain't broke, don't fix it" approach, there's also something to be said for diversification. We know an investor who for years invested only in properties in a major metropolitan area. These were C properties that the investor purchased and renovated. At the time he started purchasing these properties, that area of the city was revitalizing itself. His investments were extremely profitable and he made a conscious decision never to go outside that area with his real estate investments. Flash forward 20 years after his purchase there. The same area of the city that had once been revitalized was on a severe decline. A middle class/ lower middle class area that had once been moderately safe was now crime-ridden, drug-infested, and dangerous. Schools that were once considered good schools were now considered to be sub-par. Restaurants and other businesses that had previously flourished were struggling, some of them shuttered. The investor's investments were in severe decline, all because he had placed all of his eggs in the same basket and opted not to diversify. Again, no one is telling you that you should abandon the real estate investing philosophy that works for you, but, in the long run, you'll do best if you choose to diversify your investments.

Commercial Real Estate, Another Means to Build Your Portfolio

Commercial real estate is a different ballgame than residential real estate. For obvious reasons, commercial real estate is generally more expensive than residential real estate. Unlike residential real estate, where conventional leases are generally one year, commercial leases usually start at three years and go up to 20 years, depending on how much the property has to be customized for the tenant. If you are a real estate rental newbie, it's unlikely that you'll get into commercial real estate investing in a big way, but we'd nevertheless like to give you a brief capsule explanation of the different categories or strategies of commercial real estate investment.

1) **Core Real Estate Investments.** Core investments are known as the safest commercial real estate investments. With a core investment strategy, investors will look for stable properties in stable areas. This means high quality buildings in low vacancy areas. With a core investment strategy, investors are generally looking yield (immediate payoff) over appreciation (long-term payoff). Return on core real estate investments is generally under 10%, but investors are attracted to this strategy because it is a stable and low risk strategy.

2) **Core-Plus Investments.** As the name indicates, core-plus investments are similar to core investments, however they generally offer an opportunity to enhance returns through minor renovation or repositioning in the marketplace. These are still stable and appealing properties with a slightly higher degree of risk (possibly including some key leases that are near expiration).

3) **Value-Added Investments.** Value-added investments are the most popular strategy for commercial real estate investment. Whereas core investment strategies will normally bring less than 10% return, value-added investments will normally bring 10-15% return. Whereas the goal of a core investment strategy favors yield over appreciation, a value-added investment strategy favors appreciation over yield. In other words, a value-added investor is often OK with not receiving large profits on the property until it is either renovated, repositioned, or sold. A value-added investor is in it for the long haul and will usually hold the assets for at least five to seven years or until they've had time to enhance or reposition the property. The value-added real estate strategy is a higher risk/higher reward strategy.

Rental Properties

Lease terms and lease situations are particularly critical with a value-added strategy. For example, let's take an older industrial complex that was built in the 1970s. The complex has 12 tenants, all of whom had five-year leases when they first moved into the complex. 10 of the leases are due to expire within the next 18 months; the other two leases are for newer tenants. The building has three vacancies. Over time, it has become more difficult to lease spaces to tenants as the complex is one of the oldest within what is still a stable area. With this in mind, it looks like this complex offers a great opportunity for renovation or repositioning which would result in higher rents. On the other hand, if most of the tenants had longer times remaining on their leases, it would probably not be a good time to remodel, as you'd be spending significant remodeling dollars on tenants who are already locked into longer-term leases. So, if you're purchasing rental properties with existing tenants, you'll definitely want to take a look at the lease situation for those tenants to make sure that those leases jibe with the plans you have for the property.

4) Opportunistic. Investors who use the opportunistic investment strategy are investors who are willing to take the highest risks to achieve the highest rewards. Opportunistic properties include both existing properties and new developments. With the existing properties, those properties usually need significant work. These are normally high vacancy properties that are difficult to lease. These also might be areas that require repurposing or repositioning. As an example, what was once a huge brewery complex dating back to the late 1800s had been vacant for over 10 years after the brewery had been purchased by another brewery and the brewing plants had been consolidated. A group of investors decided to repurpose the main brewhouse as an international market which now has over 30 tenants. Obviously, this was a high risk/high reward situation as the investor group had to pump millions into the repurposing of the building and the complex. But if they are successful in turning their international market into a high-traffic destination, they'll stand to make high rewards for their strategy.

10 People You'll Need on Your Real Estate Dream Team

If you're going to build a successful real estate portfolio, you're going to have to have a "team" of people you can use throughout the process. Being a successful real estate investor requires a lot of different hats. Unlike some other profit ventures, being a "lone wolf" isn't going to work if you're a real estate investor. You're going to need the help and expertise of others in order to be successful. Here are some of the people you'll need on your real estate rental team as you work toward establishing your portfolio.

1)   Banker. Hopefully, you'll be able to establish a working relationship with a banker and he or she will come to know what you are looking for in a bank loan. Fast closing? Lower interest rates?

2)   Mortgage Broker. You'll want to find someone who is going to work for you to find the types of mortgage that you're looking for. As with most members on your team, you're going to want someone who understands your business, especially if you are purchasing properties on an on-going basis.

3)   Accountant/Bookkeeper. You'll need someone who understands real estate, including local and state real estate laws.

4)   Real Estate Attorney. There are plenty of attorneys out there, but it will behoove you to find an attorney who specializes in real estate. For example, if you have a tenant who is not paying, you'll need an attorney who is familiar with state eviction procedures.

5)   Insurance Agent. Again, you'll benefit from an agent who is willing to shop for the best policies to fit your needs.

6)   Appraiser. A good appraiser can not only give you an accurate valuation of your property, they can also suggest ways in which you can increase the value of your property.

7)   **Inspector.** A good inspector can save you tons of money. If they're thorough, they can tell you exactly what repairs will need to be made in a prospective property and how quickly those repairs will have to be made. A good inspector can be worth his or her weight in gold.

8)   **Property Manager.** If you own multiple properties or even if you own just one property and don't have the time necessary to accommodate the needs of your tenants, you'll want a good property manager. Good property managers can often mean the difference as to whether your property is rented or vacant, profitable or not profitable.

9)   **Real Estate Agent.** As you continue to build your portfolio, you'll hopefully be able to establish a solid working relationship with a real estate agent who understands the kinds of properties you are looking for. If they don't have a good idea as to what you're looking for, they'll waste a lot of your time.

10)   **Cleaning Person or Crew.** Are you going to clean a unit every time it goes vacant? Anyone who has ever done that knows that it can be a lot of work. A good cleaning crew can be a valuable asset to your real estate team.

Again, it's important to note that you should assemble a team that you can use on an on-going basis for you real estate rental properties. In doing so, it will be important for you to communicate to these team members exactly what your wishes are and what you're looking for. If you can do that, they'll became assets for you and you won't have to start at square one every time you have a need for their corresponding services. As with any team, if one of your team members is not meeting your expectations, you'll be better served to find someone else to fill their position. Your success as a real estate investor may well lie in the hands of the real estate team you assemble.

Chapter 6—The Rental to Outshine All Others

So, you're the proud owner of your very first rental property. As expected, it's going to need some work before it's rentable and you'll need to come up with a plan to get the property ready to rent. In this chapter, we'll give you a step-by-step plan on how to rehabilitate a property and get it ready to rent. We'll also tell you about some simple improvements you can make to instantly improve the value or marketability of the property.

10 Steps for Rehabbing Your Rental Property

If you're going to rehab your new rental property, you'll need to come up with a practical plan and schedule for what you're going to do and when you're going to do it. Property owners who do not get organized and instead "fly by the seat of their pants" are setting themselves up for major problems in this process. Also, as you embark on the rehabbing process for your property, you should remember that you may have to remain flexible at times. Murphy's law states that if things can go wrong, they will go wrong and you should not be surprised if you have some hiccups or hit some snags during the process. But hopefully by coming up with a detailed and practical plan before the process begins, you'll be able to minimize any potential problems. Here are some steps you can take in the rehabbing process:

1) **Assess Each Area of the Property.** Hopefully, you'll have done a preliminary assessment before you purchased the property. You'll need to go through each area of the property and determine what needs to be done to a) make the property livable and b) make it more attractive to prospective tenants. This includes a room-by-room

assessment of the interior of the property and also an assessment of the exterior of the property. If you have purchased a home with a detached garage, your assessment should include the garage. Your assessment should also include a review of the landscaping and the overall appearance of the property. In assessing the property, you'll be well served to get additional sets of eyes involved in the process. (It doesn't always take an expert to determine what they like and don't like about a property. Don't hesitate to secure the services of family and friends for this process.) As you list improvements which need to be made to the property, you should categorize those improvements as Must Make or Could Make, or whatever similar category titles work for you. It's important that you prioritize the improvements you want to make, as you may well have limited time or budget in which to make these improvements and you'll need to decide which changes can be placed on the backburner and which changes need to be done before the property is rented.

2) Make sure you have the funds available to make the changes you want to make. Hopefully you'll have done this before you purchased your property, but before you start doing any renovations, you'll need to make sure you have the funds to do so and then after you get estimates on the different projects involved in rehabbing the property, you'll then establish a budget to determine how much you are willing to spend to make the necessary changes. Again, you should already have an idea of what these changes will cost before you purchase the property. Then after you purchase the property, you can fine tune or itemize any cost estimates and determine where you'll have to cut corners in the rehabbing process.

3) Shop around. Especially for newbies, you'll have to spend some time shopping around for contractors and materials. Although no one would ever suggest that you should go with the cheapest available, especially when it comes to materials, you'll probably be very surprised at how much material costs and labor costs vary. You may be able to save thousands of dollars by doing a thorough job of shopping for both contractors and materials.

4) Line up contractors, service providers in advance. As mentioned above, it's OK to shop around for contractors and service providers, especially with your first rental property purchase. You'll want to determine pricing and also make sure you find people that you are comfortable in working with. At the same time, it won't hurt to interview multiple contractors; in the event that you have trouble with one contractor, you could move to the second contractor on the list, if necessary. And, most importantly, don't wait until the last minute to schedule contractors such as plumbers, electricians, painters, landscapers. You should remember that these people are busy working on other projects and you can't expect them to drop everything they're doing to work on your project. A successful contractor often has a busy schedule that is filled weeks, if not months, in advance. Keep this in mind when you are putting together your rehab schedule.

5) Draw up a realistic calendar. As you plan your rehab project, you'll need to develop a calendar which lists dates for all of the major tasks. You'll probably start by having contractors visit the property to quote costs for their project. At the same time you are showing them what needs to be done, you should ask them about their availability for the project. When can they start? When would they finish? This information will help you establish your calendar. And one word of caution for you as you set up your schedule. Try not to have too much going on at the property at the same time. If you have the plumber, the electrician, the cabinet installers, and the painter all there at the same time, they're likely to get in each other's way and you're likely to experience delays, or possibly even damages.

Rental Properties

6) **Track expenses.** You should be tracking your expenses throughout the process to make sure you're going to make budget. Nothing worse than getting halfway through a project, only to find out that you've overspent by a lot and you going to have to delay the project until you can come up with more money. You can use an Excel spreadsheet or Quickbooks to track your expenditures throughout the project. On the plus side, you might find that you are under budget and this might allow you to add some of the bells and whistles you have previously eliminated when you originally did your budget.

7) **Be there.** With a rehab project like this, it's going to be important for someone to be there to supervise while the work is going on. If you don't have the time to do that, you should hire or enlist the services of someone that can do that for you. We've heard stories of contractors that have ripped up floors in the wrong rooms, installed cabinets in the wrong rooms, removed the tiles from the wrong bathroom, etc. Yes, we even had a roofer whose people tore off half the shingles from the neighbor's house by mistake. These things happen and they happen often. So, it will behoove you to have someone there to supervise or answer questions while the work is going on.

8) **Have a Plan B.** What happens if one of your contractors gets delayed on another project? What happens if there is a torrential downpour when your landscaper is supposed to plant the new shrubs or the exterior painter is supposed to paint the outside of the house? What happens if one of your contractors is a total bust and you have to secure another contractor to do the job they were supposed to do? Although you can never plan for these possible hiccups, you should know that these things can and will happen. And when they do, you will have to be flexible and you'll have to move to Plan B, sometimes in urgency. (If you don't have a Plan B, you're going to have to come up with one.) This is never an easy or fun part of the process, but how

you handle it may well determine if you're going to be good at being a rental real estate property owner. Most successful rental property owners are problem solvers, and many take pride in their ability to adapt as problems arise.

9) Secure your materials. Keep your materials in a safe and secure place. Keep them out of the workers' way, so they're not impacting the way the work is being done or they are not a danger to the workers. Keep the materials in a secure place so they won't get damaged by rain or snow or so they won't get stolen.

10) Determine a sequence. As you set up a schedule for the rehabbing projects in your new rental property, it's going to be important for you to determine a practical sequence in which projects should be done and materials should be installed. A lot of this is just simple common sense. For example, don't install the new carpeting until the walls are painted, the new appliances are installed, and the laborers are done tracking through the house. Don't install new kitchen or bathroom cabinets until the painting in those rooms has been completed. Have the electricians and plumbers provide their services early in the process, unless there is a reason they should do later.

The Most Important Rehabs for All Rental Properties

In rehabbing your rental property that are a few items that should absolutely be inspected before you lease to a tenant. Some of the items are frequently overlooked; others can have a major impact on your relationship with the tenant and a major impact on your investment.

1) The Roof. We've seen instances of people who have purchased rental properties without even inspecting the roof. That's a big mistake. The roof is an essential structural component of any building and you should make sure you have it inspected, ideally before you purchase the property. If you have to add a new roof to your rental property, that's not going to be a petty cash expenditure. You should know the condition of your roof, so you can plan accordingly for any repairs that need to be done. A faulty roof cannot be ignored and you'll be risking the value of your investment if you don't make sure the roof remains in good condition.

2)   Carpeting, Painting. Common, relatively inexpensive things that are normally included in any rehab project. If you have shabby carpeting or painting, it's likely to impact your ability to lease the property, as it's one of the first things that prospective tenants see.

3)   Windows. Like roofs, not an inexpensive proposition. From an investment standpoint, you'll want to make sure your property has upgraded windows as it enhances the value of your property. Also, from a tenant standpoint, a good set of windows can help substantially with the insulation of the house and will reduce heating and air conditioning bills.

4)   Electrical. 200 amp panels recommended, as they are not much more expensive than 100 amp panels.

5)   Heating/Air Conditioning/Vents. It's a good idea to have these inspected at least once a year, even when the property is occupied. Heating and air conditioning systems are not cheap and you'll want to make sure they are kept in good condition. You can't expect that your tenants will do so. We've heard stories of properties that have had fires because dryer vents were clogged. Routine maintenance can easily prevent major problems.

6) **Furnace.** Along the same lines, you need to keep tabs on the furnace in your property. An average furnace will last 10-15 years and, as you might expect, they are somewhat expensive. You'll be well served if you know what condition your furnace is in and when you might need another, so you can plan accordingly. You'll also want to make sure that you or your tenant is changing filters in your furnace regularly, as clogged furnace filters can do some serious damage.

7) **Sewer system/plumbing.** Make sure you monitor the sewer system in your property. A sewer backup can cause some serious damage to the property. You should certainly have the sewer lines inspected and checked at the outset of any rehab project. And then have them checked regularly, depending on how likely they are to get clogged. For example, someone who owns a home with a lot of trees on the property may find that they have tree roots that clog the sewer pipes regularly. If you know this, you can schedule routine maintenance on a regular basis to prevent any major problems. At the same time you're checking the sewer system, it's probably a good idea to check all the drains and the garbage disposal. If you can make sure these things are clear before your tenant moves in, you may be able to eliminate middle-of-the-night calls informing you of these problems.

8) **Water heaters.** Water heaters are fairly inexpensive. They'll normally last 8 to 12 years, depending on how hard the water is in your area and how good the water heater is. If your water heater is approaching this age, it's probably a good idea to start thinking about a new one.

Home Improvements to Instantly Boost the Value of Your Property

Rental Properties

In the previous section, we focused on functional and structural items which are strongly recommended for any rental rehab project. Now let's take a look at some of the "funner" stuff, things you can do to enhance the cosmetic value, the eye appeal, and the ultimate value of your property. You'll note that many of these cosmetic enhancements are not major renovation or expensive projects. With many of these recommendations, you'll find that you can boost the value or appeal of your property without breaking the bank.

1) **Bathroom facelift.** Regardless of how small it is, the bathroom is considered one of the focal points of any home. Bathroom upgrades including re-tiling, re-caulking, replacing or re-glazing tubs or showers, or a new vanity with modern lighting are all things you can do to upgrade your bathrooms. Research shows that bathroom upgrades can add more to the value of a residential property than any other room. The payback on bathroom upgrades is more than double the amount invested in the upgrade.

2) **Landscape redesign.** Another eye appeal project which can add substantial and immediate value to a property. Things such as trimming shrubs and trees, weeding, and adding new plants or bushes can easily add to the value and the curb appeal of a property.

3) **Minor kitchen remodel.** You don't have to spend a fortune to increase the eye appeal of your kitchen. Simple things such as updated appliances, new counter tops, and new cabinet facings can easily increase the appeal of your kitchen. New floor tiles and new wallpaper are also things that can be done inexpensively to enhance your kitchen.

4) **Exterior improvements.** Besides some landscaping enhancements, you can increase the curb appeal of your home with a new paint job, new siding, new trim, or a new front door.

5) **Bedroom conversion.** Is there a marginal, non-essential room in the house that you can convert to another bedroom? Even if it is a small bedroom, that extra bedroom can add substantially to the value of a home.

All of the above-mentioned renovations can add substantially to the eye appeal of your home, making it easier to rent. As most homes are now viewed online before a potential renter even inquires about them, eye appeal/curb appeal is more important than ever. If you don't have an attractive property, it's going to be difficult to even get potential renters to visit your property. And from a long-term standpoint, these cosmetic enhancements can also add financial value to your home many times over. For each of the five renovations listed above, the lowest expected payback on the investment is in the 90th percentile. This means that with whatever you invest in any of these areas, you should be able to almost double your investment as it adds to the value of your property.

Chapter 7—Managing Your Rental

OK, you're done rehabbing your rental property. Now it's time to rent the property. Some property owners make the mistake of thinking that most of their work is done and most of their problems are over once they've finished preparing their property for rental. That might well be a drastic misassumption. If you aren't renting to the right people, your problems might just be starting and you might be jeopardizing all of the time and money you've already spent on the property. Getting good tenants into your properties is extremely important. Once the property is ready, your ability to get good tenants may well be the key to whether your property is profitable or not. With this in mind, we have some solid recommendations on what you can do to minimize tenant problems.

Finding Great Tenants for Your Rental

1) **Don't discriminate.** Before we get into the basics of what you should do to find great tenants, we should caution you not to discriminate. There are federal laws that prohibit discrimination and you'll need to adhere to these regulations when renting your property. We've read numerous stories of landlords who have been sued for their discriminatory practices and you won't want to be one of those people. Settlement amounts for these lawsuits are sometimes more that the value of the property itself, so we certainly implore you not to discriminate in renting your properties.

The Fair Housing Act prohibits discrimination in the following areas:

--Race or color

Rental Properties

--Religion

--National origin

--Sex

--Familial status. (You can't discriminate against families with kids.)

--Disability

2) Create a detailed rental application. Leasing a property is serious business and you should not hesitate to use a detailed rental application that will help you gather the information you'll need to determine whether to rent to the applicant or not. Included in the application should be the following items:

a) Personal references. Ask for two or three personal references, preferably non-family references. Then you need to make sure that you follow up with these references before you rent to the applicant. When you are talking to these references, we suggest that one of the questions you ask them if the tenant has told them why they are moving and then make sure that matches what he is telling you.

b) Employment history. This information might tell you something as to how stable the applicant is. If they've done a lot of job switching or there are an unusual number of employment gaps, this might be an indicator that they won't be a stable tenant. And with employment history, you'll probably be well served to check that the history listed on the application is correct. It's not all that unusual for people to fabricate information on rental applications.

c) Previous rental history. It's possible that your applicant won't have any rental history. (i.e.—recent high school or college grad, retired couple who have downsized, etc.) However, if a history is listed, you'll do well to contact the previous landlords. Instead of just confirming residency, you should also ask other questions that might help you in determining whether the applicant will be a good tenant. Those questions might include: Did they pay their rent on time? Were they clean? Respectful to neighbors and staff? Did they leave the unit in good condition when they vacated? Did they give the required notice before moving out? Did any of the neighbors complain about them? Did they require an unusual amount of attention as a tenant? Would you lease to them again?

d) Credit checks. Run a credit check on your prospective tenant and take it seriously. Some landlords set a credit score limit in renting to tenants. A required credit score of 650 is a common requirement. If the candidate seems like a decent candidate, but the credit score isn't what you'd like it to be, you might ask if there is an explanation for the low score. Credit checks will also tell you how much debt the applicant has (see income-to-debt ratio note in the following verify income category), whether he or she has been evicted from a previous property, and whether he or she has any judgments against them.

e) Verify income. It's not unusual for rental applicants to fudge on their stated income, so it will behoove you to take the time to verify their income. Contact their current employer and verify income, length of employment, standing with the company, and attendance record. As a rule of thumb, you'll want to find a tenant whose monthly income is three times the proposed rent amount. There are exceptions to this, of course, such as retired couples who may have limited income, but have nest eggs that can easily accommodate the rent amounts.

When we say that ideally a tenant should have income which is three times his rent amount, we should also harken back to the credit check/credit score, where you should make a note to check the applicant's income-to-debt ratio. For example, you might have one applicant who has an income of $3000 a month; another who has an income of $2500 a month. You might think that the higher-earning candidate is always the better candidate, but that's not always the case.

Rental Properties

Maybe the higher-earning candidate has debt payments totaling $1500 a month, while the lower-earning candidate has no debts at all, except for a nominal car payment. In this instance, the lower-earning candidate might be a better candidate, at least from a financial standpoint.

f) Criminal background check. Criminal history is one of the most "lied about" things on job and rental applications. So, we highly recommend that you do a criminal background check on any prospective tenant that you're interested in. Doing a criminal background check yourself can be very time-consuming, so you may want to use a tenant screening company to do this for you.

Use the information you collect to evaluate the tenant realistically. You should obviously have more concerns about a tenant who has had drug-dealing or sexual assault charges than someone who has multiple speeding tickets. Also, pay attention to when the crimes were committed. Is it a 50-year old man who had some drunk driving charges in his 20s and hasn't had anything since? Or has he had more recent offenses? This information may well make a difference as to whether your prospective tenant is a good candidate or not.

A couple of other quick notes about criminal background checks: If you hire a tenant screening company to provide a background check for you, most of these companies will do a federal and statewide record search, a county search, a Department of Corrections search, and a sexual offender database search. Although this is public information, it can be difficult and time-consuming to gather if you haven't done it before; the cost to use a tenant screening company is nominal. (There is no nationwide criminal database, so criminal background checks are not as thorough or as simple as you might thing they would be.) Also, we should mention that some states, including California, prohibit landlords from discriminating against prospective tenants who have committed certain types of crimes. This means that you'll want to become familiar with whatever your local laws are before you rule out a tenant due to criminal history. That being said, certain past criminal history, including domestic assault, drug- or human-trafficking, drug-dealing, etc., are all activities that should raise immediate red flags for landlords.

g) Face-to-face; gut instinct. When you show your property to your prospective tenants, you should make an effort to get to know them. Hopefully, you can use your meeting with them to start to establish a relationship and maybe get a gut feel as to whether they will be a good tenant or not. And don't hesitate to ask them questions which might help you in determining whether they are a good candidate. Any questions should obviously be appropriate and not too personal (you're not conducting an interrogation), but you might be able to secure some information which will be helpful in evaluating the candidate. Here are some questions you might ask an applicant: Why are you looking to move? Where do you live now? Have you ever rented before? Have you ever had a problem with a landlord before? If you are accepted to rent the property, do you have any idea as to how long you might rent it? What do you do for a living? Do you smoke or have pets? Do you think you'll be a good tenant?

You'll note that some of these questions will be the same questions that are asked on your application form. That's OK. You may be surprised to find out that sometimes the answers you get on an application form don't jibe with the answers to the same questions in a face-to-face meeting. If so, that might indicate some red flags.

Also, in starting to establish a relationship with a possible tenant, you'll then find it easier to go back to them if any questions should arise from their credit check, their reference check, their background check, etc. You might be able to determine how forthcoming they will be, for example, if you ask them why their credit score is "iffy". Maybe there is a logical explanation for their credit score. If everything seems to fit, except maybe one thing, don't hesitate to ask the applicant for an explanation…unless you have many other legitimate applicants for the same property. Either way, the bottom line is that you should use your face-to-face interaction with the prospective tenant to get a feel as to whether they'll be a good tenant. Gut instinct won't trump some of the facts you secure regarding your applicant, however it does count for something and it might be the difference-maker in choosing one candidate over another.

And before we leave this topic, we should mention how important it is to keep good tenants once you have them. You can do this by responding promptly to any tenant requests or questions and also by establishing an open line of communication with them. Let them know that you are there to help them with their needs and it won't hurt to ask them occasionally if they are satisfied with the rental or if they have any feedback regarding the property. If you don't know it already, you'll find out soon…good tenants can make your life a whole lot easier and they can make the difference between a profitable property and an unprofitable property.

We encourage to treat your tenants just as if you would treat a valued customer in any other business. We know successful landlords who send birthday cards, holiday cards, and thank you cards to tenants. We also know landlords who have "exit interviews" with tenants who are vacating the property. In doing so, they'll look for feedback regarding the property. The feedback provided may be helpful to the landlord in future endeavors. Either way, you should always remember that the better the relationship you can develop with your tenant, the more likely it will be for them to continue to rent from you. As you're well aware, any time you have to turn over a lease, you're going to have to spend time to find a new tenant and you also make have some vacancy time in which the property is draining your bank account instead of adding to it.

Strategies for Managing Rental Property

It probably won't surprise you when we point out that if you don't manage a property correctly, that property can turn into a nightmare for you. Instead of being the profit center you hope it to be, it can become a giant money pit and leave you wondering why you ever decided to get into rental real estate. Thankfully, there are a number of different ways you can manage a property successfully. Some rental property owners will be successful with a strictly hands-on approach. Other owners will be successful by outsourcing everything. And others will be successful with a mix of hands-on and outsourcing.

Before you get into these different strategies, it's important to explain the three different areas of managing a property. You'll need to focus on these three areas if you want to achieve maximum profit potential with your rental properties.

1) **Manage tenants.** As a rental property owner, you or whoever you hire to do so is going to be responsible for managing tenants. The task of managing tenants includes leasing the property (and determining the viability of tenants), collecting rent, and developing/implementing/updating lease agreements. It also involves handling tenant requests (repair requests and information requests) promptly, coordinating move in and move out dates, and, unfortunately, sometimes evictions.

2) **Managing the property for maintenance and inspections.** As a landlord you'll also be responsible for the maintenance and the upkeep of the property. With commercial property or multi-unit properties, this may include the responsibilities of arranging for common area maintenance (grass cutting and landscaping, janitorial services (including restrooms), garbage collection, snow removal, heat and running water, roof leaks, etc. Obviously, residential properties will include less responsibility. In some residential renter agreements, tenants may be responsible for their own snow shoveling, lawn mowing, garbage collection, etc. Unfortunately, with maintenance, you usually won't be able to plan in advance. Problems are likely to spring up at the most unlikely of times, and you'll have to make sure that you or whoever you hire to handle these tasks will be available at "the drop of a dime". Also, you should know that you will have to arrange to accommodate inspections of your property. Local inspectors may want to inspect your property to make sure it meets all health and safety codes, including fire codes. Mortgage and insurance companies may want to inspect the property to make sure that the property corresponds with the amounts they are lending or for which they are insuring.

3) **Managing finances.** As a rental property owner, it's going to be important for you to keep a constant handle on how much money is coming in and how much is going out. As we've said before, being a rental property owner is not a hobby, and you'll want to make sure that your properties are as profitable as possible. Rental property financial responsibilities include collecting rent from tenants and then making payments to the various parties involved, including mortgage payments, insurance, and taxes. It also may include making utility payments and paying any fees and fines.

As a landlord, you're going to have to pay attention to all three of these areas. Although it is natural for a person to drift toward the tasks they enjoy doing and wander away from those tasks they don't enjoy, you are going to have to make sure that you are not ignoring any of these areas of responsibility. If you do neglect any of these areas, you're likely to pay the consequences and your neglect will most certainly impact the profitability of your property. That being said, some landlords will make it a point to outsource any of the responsibilities they have no interest in doing, as they are aware that they will tend to neglect these areas. Now that we've outlined the different responsibilities of owning a property, it's time to look at three different strategies to use in managing properties.

The Hands-on/Do-it-Yourself Strategy. If you intend to be a hands-on/do-it-yourself landlord, you're going to have to be a person of many different hats. Landlords will opt for the hands-on strategy for a number of reasons, including total control, the ability to keep costs at a minimum, and the ability to identify and solve problems immediately. This is a lot easier for single unit or owner-occupied properties; it's a lot more difficult for commercial or larger multi-unit properties.

The downside of a hands-on management approach is that you may be attempting to do some things that you're really not knowledgeable enough to do. For example, a rental property owner who sets out to do everything involved may have to be an accounting expert, a legal expert, a maintenance expert (roofer, electrician, plumber). It's likely that you are still going to have to outsource some of the responsibilities involved in being a rental property owner, and you shouldn't feel bad about that. It's normal. In being a hands-on owner, you're likely going to have to be available 24/7/365, and, as mentioned above, you're not going to be able to control when problems arise. Some people find this overwhelming and that's why many owners end up outsourcing certain tasks and responsibilities. Other owners soon find that their time can be more valuably spent doing other things and they'll then outsource certain tasks. As an example, maybe you decide to draft your own lease agreement without the assistance or expertise of a real estate attorney. You could in fact find examples on the internet and then draft your own agreement. But you'll also have to make sure you are familiar with local leasing laws and regulations, which are different in individual states. By the time you finish researching rental agreements, you may find out that you would have been better off hiring a real estate attorney. Or maybe you miss one of the local laws in your agreement and find out later that this omission has left an expensive loophole in your agreement. Bottom line is that you'll have to decide which tasks you're capable of performing and which tasks you're willing to take the time to perform. In some instances, you'll decide that you'll want to outsource some of these responsibilities.

As you can see from the above description, a hands-on management approach is mostly suited toward a landlord who either owns a small number of properties, who has a lot of experience managing properties, or who wants total control in managing those properties.

The Mixed Responsibility Strategy. Most landlords, even those on the smaller spectrum, tend to use a mixed responsibility strategy in managing their properties. We touched on some of this above when we described the possible cons of trying to do everything yourself. Are you a legal expert? An accounting expert? A plumber? An electrician? A roofer? What if you get caught up in an expensive legal battle because you tried to draft your own rental agreement and were not aware of important local rules and regulations? What if you miss a key loophole in paying your taxes because you tried to do your own accounting instead of hiring an accounting expert? You get the picture…sometimes we can get into trouble by trying to be all things to all people. We'll be better served to outsource responsibilities that are outside our areas of expertise or interest.

The biggest benefits of using a mixed responsibility strategy are that you'll free up some of your time and you'll also be assured that your protecting your physical and financial assets by using experts. On the negative side, you'll lose some control and you will be relying on others, placing your reputation as a landlord in the hands of others. So, if you are building your rental portfolio, and you're past the stage of owning your first rental property, the mixed responsibility strategy is probably best for you. The average landlord handles some responsibilities himself and farms out other responsibilities to others.

Outsource Management Completely. There are a number of reasons why rental property owners will opt to outsource all management responsibilities. Some owners will do so because they own non-local properties and it's simply not logistically feasible for them to be hands-on property owners. Some owners own so many properties that they can't be involved on a hands-on basis. And finally, some investors have real estate investments as just a part of their total investments and they simply don't have the time to be hands-on managers.

Most of the landlords who outsource management responsibilities will either hire managers for their properties or they will utilize a management company. Managers or management companies should be able to perform or arrange for all of the tasks that are involved in managing the property: securing and screening tenants, arranging for repairs, coordinating move ins and move outs, collecting rents, pursuing delayed rents, evictions, coordinating routine maintenance and long-term maintenance and upgrades. A good manager or management company should obviously have a good working relationship with the owner of the property. It's obvious that mismanagement of any property could result in the demise of that property.

The upside of hiring a manager or a management company for your properties will be that you will free up a lot of your time. You won't be the one getting the phone calls in the middle of the night from tenants telling you their heat isn't working. And, if you do your due diligence in hiring a good manager or a good management company, you'll know that you'll be using experts in managing these properties instead of trying to wear hats that don't fit you.

The downsides of outsourcing everything involve costs and control. Especially if you are a small-time rental property owner, you're going to have to be aware that a manager, management company, or any of the companies you hire to assist with the responsibilities of owning a rental property (attorneys, accountants, plumbers, electricians) are going to cost money. And, the money you pay them will have an influence on your profitability. That being said, not hiring good managers or other experts in their field, may impact your property's ability to be successful in the long term.

12 Must-Know Tips from Rental Property Experts

Although we've included plenty of tips throughout this book on how to manage your rental properties, we have some additional tips to offer or to expand upon:

1) Use professional photographs to market your property. You can't derive any rental income from your property if you can't rent it. The importance of good photographs is often underestimated in marketing a property. It's no secret that most prospective tenants will want to view the property and the unit before deciding whether they will visit the property. In order not to get ruled out immediately, you'll want to make sure that you are using attractive photos that properly highlight the property. In advertising your property online, show as many photos as possible. Show each room in the property and also the exterior of the property. If the property has any unique features, show closeup photos of those features. On the other hand, try not to highlight outdated features. Do whatever is possible to show a clean and uncluttered property. Remember that when prospective tenants view your property online, they'll likely be comparing against photos of other properties. Some property owners hire professional photographers to use in marketing their properties. In advertising your rental property, you'll want to make sure it stands out from other properties in the same rental category.

2) Consider allowing pets. We've all heard horror stories about how a pet can demolish a residence. But then again, some people demolish their residences also. As homeownership is dwindling, you should know that an open pet policy, usually for dogs and cats, might increase the marketability of your property. You can restrict pet occupancy as you see fit (by limiting the number of pets or the size of pets), and you can even seek an additional deposit or an additional rental fee for a pet. Obviously, when you say you allow cats in the unit, you won't want the tenant to have tigers or lions in there. Ha. And many property owners will restrict dog size to medium or small. Great Danes not allowed! If you're having difficulty marketing and renting your property, this might be an option to consider. We know a rental property owner who rents to a lot of baby boomers who have previously owned homes and are downsizing. He does well in allowing pets in his properties, making them available to a lot more prospective tenants.

3) Install smart locks in your rentals. If you're not familiar with smart locks, they are electronic devices which allow keyless entry into a property through use of a smartphone. Although there is obviously a cost involved in installing keyless entry, research shows that these costs typically pay for themselves within seven months of the expenditure. As competitive as the rental market can be, time is money when it comes to leasing properties. When a tenant asks you to show a property and you're not able to accommodate them immediately because of schedule conflicts, they may move on to the next property and you may lose that prospective tenant. Or if you are delayed in showing them the property, it's likely that the lease may be delayed. Studies show that properties with smart locks lease 3-7 days faster than properties with traditional locks. Smart locks are not only safer and more convenient for tenants, they also add to the value of the property and they enable self-showings in which the landlord or the manager don't have to be present.

4)   Landscaping/simple updating. Curb appeal/eye appeal are extremely important. There are many inexpensive ways you can make your property more attractive to prospective tenants. Upon visiting your property, any prospective tenant will see the exterior of your home before they see the interior. If they are already "turned off" before they see the inside of the place, you may have already lost your chance to rent the property. Many landscaping changes can be done on a modest budget. These changes will not just increase the marketability of the property, they will also increase the overall value of the property. Same goes for any features in your property that are noticeably outdated. Features such a granite kitchen counter tops, stainless steel kitchen sinks, well-lit bathrooms, and updated appliances can easily increase the marketability of the property without costing you a fortune.

5)   Rental walk-through. Once you have rented the property, it will behoove you are your property manager to do an immediate walk-through with the new tenant. This walk-through will allow you to identify any immediate concerns that the tenant has. It will also allow you to document any possible concerns. It's better to identify these concerns at the outset of the lease, so any required changes can be addressed immediately. Also, it is better to pinpoint any problems at the beginning of the lease instead of at the end. For example, if you missed some carpet stains at the outset of the lease (maybe the guy installing the new water heater had some leakage when he removed the old water heater), those stains should be documented and photographed on the walk-through, so this will not be a point of contention at the end of the lease when the deposit refund comes into question. These things should always be documented, because by the time you hit the end of the lease, you may well have forgotten about these problems until the tenant brings them up again.

6)   Upgrading when the property is vacant. Whenever possible, you should do your upgrading between leases or whenever the property is vacant. Obviously, you won't want to inconvenience your current tenants with upgrades, if those upgrades can wait and are not emergency upgrades. And we should also mention that it is important for you to take the time to reevaluate your property between every tenant and, if the unit needs upgrading or renovation, then you may be able to delay the start date of the new lease while you make the renovations.

7)   Attend to tenant concerns immediately. We mentioned this briefly before, but it's going to be important for you as a landlord to always address tenant concerns and requests immediately. If a tenant thinks that you are lackadaisical concerning their requests, they may get the feeling that you don't care and you're only interested in taking their money at the end of each month. If the tenant requests a repair and you can't get someone there to rectify the problem immediately, keep your client posted on exactly when they might expect the problem to be fixed. Again, a reminder, tenants who feel that a landlord is attentive to their needs are much more likely to extend their leases.

8)   Express appreciation. A landlord/tenant relationship should be a two-way street and you should make a point to tell your tenants how much you appreciate them (if, in fact, you do). Some landlords send birthday cards, holiday cards, or thank you cards to tenants. Other landlords will send handwritten notes telling the appropriate tenants how much they always appreciate their prompt rental payments or how they appreciate how they always keep the property clean and in good condition. Again, a tenant who feels appreciated is more likely to extend the lease.

9) Require renter's insurance. This is something that often gets overlooked by landlords. You'll do well to require your renter to have renter's insurance and to demand proof of that insurance. You might think that a tenant is the only one who can benefit from his own insurance. Well, you can also benefit. Let's say that the tenant leaves the bathtub faucet running and floods the unit…or they leave the stove on while they are taking a phone call and a fire results. Or, what happens if your tenant totally trashes the unit, far exceeding the security deposit you have for that unit? In these instances, you will be able to benefit from your tenant's insurance.

10) Keep security deposits separate. Speaking of security deposits, please remember that when a tenant makes a security deposit, that's not your money and you will be wise to keep that money separate and in escrow. If you are ever unable to refund the security deposit at the end of the lease, you are likely to be subject to penalties and fines which well exceed the security deposit amounts.

11) Use property management software. One lost receipt can cost you a possible tax deduction. A lost or misplaced lease can cost you months in eviction court proceedings. Technology can help you manage your property. Instead of having misplaced notes or paperwork in multiple areas of your office, you can have it all in one place. You can use technology to keep track of your property listing, to keep track of rental payments and repair requests and history, signed leases, and tenant screenings. It's good to have all this information in the same place. A property management software program can help you do that.

12) Be willing to make concessions and extend lease terms to good tenants. As mentioned before, finding good tenants can be a trying and difficult task. So, once you find a good tenant, you'll want to work hard to keep them. A vacant property is going to cost you money, even if it is only vacant a month. Along the same lines, you'll have to spend additional time in securing a new tenant, who may not be a good tenant like the last one was.

We've previously mentioned the importance of promptly addressing tenant requests and also establishing a good line of communication with your tenants. Another way to keep good tenants is to offer to extend them or to make concessions if they extend their lease. We've known landlords who have had a lot of success in making or offering renewal concessions. Examples of concessions might be a free month's rent with minimum extension of 12 months or more, no rental increase if lease is extended by a specified date, or, if you live in a northern area and a lease is due to expire during the winter season, you might offer to extend the lease at the same rate for just a few months. This will allow your tenant to vacate at a time when the weather is more conducive to a move and it will allow you as the landlord a better time to find a new tenant, when the rental market is more active. Again, open lines of communication with a tenant can make your job as a landlord a lot easier. Keep in touch with your tenant to find out what their intentions are when the lease expires. This will help you from a planning standpoint and it may also help you get a feel for whether your tenant is even open to an extension.

In a similar vein, if rental rates in your market have been decreasing, and your lease rate is now above market rate, offering a free month's rent or even half a month's rent for an extension might increase your chances for an extension and keep your tenant from shopping other properties.

Chapter 8—Precautions

If you're thinking of getting into the real estate rental business, you've most likely heard some tremendous success stories along the way. Those stories may have amplified your interest in the business. That being said, you need to also be aware of the possible pitfalls of the business. Human nature tells us that investors are not as quick to tell horror stories as they are to tell success stories. Any business that has tremendous success also probably has some serious risks. This is the case with the real estate rental business. We would never attempt to put a damper on your interest to enter the industry, but we want to remind you to go into the real estate rental business with your eyes wide open, just as you would within any other business. Here are some common reasons why rental property investors fail:

1) Underestimating overall startup capital. Some investors make the mistake of underestimating what their startup costs will be for a rental property. They'll look at the sell price of the property itself, and then they'll underestimate the costs to renovate that property or the cost to make it marketable. Please know that although the sell price of the property may be the main expense, you'll have to have enough money to make the property marketable. You'll be well served to do the research on renovation costs before you purchase the property. You'll also do well to pad the amounts you estimate, so you have an extra cushion in there for projects you may have overlooked or cost estimates that come in higher than originally quoted.

We always caution rental property investors not to think that their spending stops with the closing on the property. For some property owners, that's when the spending starts. Even if the property you purchase is in good condition, you may have to do some updates to bring your property up to code, especially if you are going from what was an owner-occupied property to a rental property. Many states and municipalities have different regulations for rental properties and you'll be well-served to know what the rules are in your state and municipality. If you don't, you could be in for some expensive surprises.

2) **Underestimating or not planning for unexpected/emergency repairs.** This is another pitfall that can lead to failure. The furnace you thought had three to five more years in it goes out and you receive a late-night call on a cold evening from your tenant telling you that he now has no heat. You have to contact and hire a heating company immediately to find out what the problem is. The technician you hire tells you that your furnace is shot and you'll have to get a new one. New furnaces are not cheap and you'll have to have access to immediate cash for the new furnace and installation. Either that, or you could face legal action from a disgruntled tenant. You get the picture. If you're going to get involved in the rental property business, you're going to have to have contingency funds or funding to cover unexpected and sometimes substantial emergencies.

3) **Deadbeat Tenants/Problem Tenants.** OK, you've purchased your first rental property and spent two months rehabbing it and another month securing a tenant for the property. The monthly rent arrives on time each of the first three months, but then you don't receive the rent for the fourth month. You've had a difficult time reaching the tenant and when you finally reach him, he informs you that they've had some family emergencies and he's been unable to come up with the funds for this month's rent. He'll try to get you some money soon, but things aren't looking promising as he was laid off from his job soon after they moved into the rental. Well, you certainly didn't expect that.

Rental Properties

Now, you'll quickly have to become familiar with the eviction process. Not only will you be missing the income you expected from the rental, you now might have to hire an attorney to evict the tenant. And how long before you can evict the tenant? States have different laws regarding tenant eviction and some of those laws allow tenants to stay well past their welcome. And then you'll have to spend time marketing and leasing the property again. It might take you 30-60 days past the eviction to lease the property again. You get the picture. You'll need to have contingency funds to account for deadbeat tenants. Yes, you can reduce the chances of a deadbeat tenant by vetting that tenant properly before you lease them the property, but even with that, life happens and you may be presented with tenants who are no longer able to pay their rent.

We heard an interesting story from a first-time rental property investor who decided to rent out his condo after he purchased a new home. He rented his condo to a man and his girlfriend. The tenant was a well-paid attorney at a reputable law firm. The girlfriend, who was not on the lease, had a fledgling modeling career. Rent payments from this tenant were always prompt until they stopped completely five months into the lease. In contacting the tenant, the landlord was told that the man and his girlfriend had had a blowout and the man was now living with a friend of his instead of living in the rental unit. The girlfriend, now apparently the ex-girlfriend, had continued to live in the rental unit after the fight.

The tenant, an attorney, stated that he no longer intended to make payments (even though he had a solid 12-month lease, and he would not be living there. If his ex-girlfriend wanted to pick up the lease, that would be fine with him. Left to fend for himself against a tenant who was an attorney, the landlord knew he was in the middle of a fiasco. He did a surprise inspection on the property and found out that the front door of the condo had extensive damage, probably from someone who attempted to break down a door in a domestic fight. Upon entering the unit, he also found that there were cats in the unit despite that fact that pets were not allowed in the lease agreement. He also noted substantial carpet damage from what looked to be hair dye.

Who woulda thunk it? The landlord had vetted his tenant properly, he had rented to a party who could easily pay the monthly rent and someone who seemed likely to be a tenant who would care for the property. Yet, now here he was, having to file legal proceedings against his attorney tenant. When the landlord contacted the girlfriend, he found that she was between modeling gigs and couldn't pay the entire amount of the rent because her ex was refusing to help her. She offered to pay half the amount of the rent. This was unacceptable to the landlord and he knew that he'd have to hire an attorney to initiate legal proceedings against his tenant. Thankfully, the woman agreed to move out at the end of the month, so he wouldn't have to evict her.

Yes, it's a horror story, but it does have a "happy" ending. Just before the landlord was about to initiate illegal proceedings against his deadbeat attorney tenant, he mentioned the problem to his racquetball buddy, a corporate attorney for the company the landlord worked for. Ironically, the corporate attorney had a close working relationship with the law firm that the deadbeat tenant worked for. The corporate attorney called a partner at the law firm the deadbeat worked for. The same day, the deadbeat attorney delivered a check for the past due amount and all the remaining months on the lease. The landlord later found out that the partner at the law firm of the deadbeat had read the riot act to the deadbeat and told him that if he ever expected to make partner someday, he'd be well-advised not to tarnish the sterling reputation of the law firm. With that said, the deadbeat delivered a large check covering the remaining months of the lease and he also offered to pay for the damaged door and carpeting. Bottom line, this first-time landlord got lucky. It was pure happenstance that his problem was solved as easily as it was. In most instances, the landlord would have been left "holding the bag", never seeing the remaining months owed on the lease.

This story illustrates two possible areas which can cause tenants to fail: tenant non-payment and property damage. Most of you have heard nightmarish stories about rental units which have been left in disarray by tenants. A moneycrashers.com blog told the story of a landlord who rented to a trio of college students. Again, upon non-payment, the landlord did an inspection of the property. He found a large hole in the ceiling separating the second floor from the ground floor. A large fireman's pole had been haphazardly installed to allow the tenants quick access from the upper floor to the bottom floor. The graffiti which now filled the walls of the until was the least of the landlord's concerns.

4) Evictions. If you're under the impression that evictions are simple, you've got another thing coming. Evictions can be expensive and time consuming. First, you may find out that the courts are backed up and you may have to wait a while for a court date. Presuming that you win the case and the court approves the eviction notice, you might then have to wait a while for the sheriff or a member of law enforcement to accompany you when you execute the eviction. You may then find that belongings have been left behind. Most state laws will not allow you to discard those belongings for a certain amount of time and you may have to pay to store them. Besides that, it shouldn't surprise anyone that vacated properties are not always left in the best of condition and you may well have to spend a lot of time and effort cleaning the unit or making damage repairs to the unit. And then there's the fact that eviction of a tenant can take up to 90 days or more in some states or municipalities that require multiple steps for eviction. So, you can see how evictions can bring down landlords. In the property rental business, time is money, and the time and money you spend in evicting a tenant can have a significant impact on your property rental business.

5) Managing finances. Anyone who is in the rental property business can tell you that a landlord's finances don't stay constant. You can sit down at the beginning of the year and make projections for your property or properties, but you'll find that your monthly projections are seldomly going to be what you thought they would be. Things will likely be going well if your units are rented, you don't have any vacancies, your tenants are paying on time, and no major repairs are necessary. But what if you have say five units and two of them have vacancies? Are you prepared for that financially? Whether you are experiencing feast or famine with your real estate real business, you'll need to be disciplined in your finances. Even if things are going extremely well, you can't be sure when your property or properties will require major repairs or vacancies. You'll need to account for these down times by accumulating a sufficient contingency fund when times are good. In the above section on evictions, you saw how long an eviction could take. You'll want to make sure you have the funds to "ride out the storm" in the event that happens. Same goes for vacancies and difficulty in renting out a unit; same goes for major repairs. Do you have the cash on hand to replace a furnace if it goes out? These are all things to consider as a landlord.

6) Keep your properties safe and in good condition. If you have a tenant who gets injured on your property, it's likely that you'll get sued. Even if your homeowner's insurance covers your liability, you'll probably still have to hire an attorney to represent you. Even with a homeowner's policy, you'll be expected to keep your property safe and in working order. As a landlord, it will behoove you to know what your local safety codes are and then follow those codes. We've heard stories of landlords who have been sued for large amounts because they weren't following local safety codes, either because they didn't know those codes or because they ignored those codes.

7) **Taxes.** Don't overlook property taxes. Make sure you understand the impact that property taxes can have on your property and then plan and save accordingly. It shouldn't surprise anyone to find out that property taxes can have a major impact on the bottom line of your business. By knowing these numbers in advance, you should be able to incorporate them in the rental fees to your tenants.

The above cautionary tales are certainly not meant to scare you away from buying rental properties. Buying and owning rental properties can be a very lucrative business…if done correctly. It's not all fun and games and it should never be considered a hobby. It's serious business and it's not for everyone. But if you're willing to do your homework and work diligently to become a good landlord, you'll have the opportunity to make money in the rental property business.

Good reasons to let go of rental property.

Many rental property investors wonder about when it's a good time to sell the rental property they own. There are a number of situations which are conducive toward selling your property:

1) **You can get more than you paid for it.** Your investment strategy will have an impact on whether you should sell a property that has appreciated. If the property has appreciated in value and it's bringing in profits as a rental property, you'll have to decide whether you want to sell it at any given time. Some investors will want to sell the property and cash in their chips while they can; others will prefer the monthly income they obtain from the property and will choose to hang on to the property. It should be noted that if you sell an appreciated property, you'll know exactly what you're getting for that property. If you hang on to it, you won't know if it will appreciate or depreciate in value; you also won't know if it will remain as a steady rental profit center, depending on the area it's in and the inventory of rental properties in that area.

2) **Negative cash flow.** The late Kenny Rogers had a song that said, "You gotta know when to hold 'em, know when to fold 'em, know when to walk away, know when to run". Although those lines from his song weren't meant to describe rental properties, those lines certainly apply to rental property. If you have a property that is not making you money, it's probably time to unload it…unless you have absolute indicators that you'll be able to turn it around quickly. Some real estate investors get caught up in the idea that maybe the negative cash flow properties will change in the future or they can't let go of an emotional attachment they have to those properties. We need to remember that one of the main reasons people invest in rental property is to make money. If you have a property that is not making money, then it's probably time to fold and use the money from the sale to invest in something more profitable.

3) **A strong seller's market.** If you have a market that has a low inventory of rental properties in your area and a low mortgage rate for buyers, it's a good time to look at the possibility of selling your property. We all know that the real estate economy (and the general economy) is cyclical and you'll be well-served if you sell your property when the factors work to your advantage.

4) **The property no longer fits your plans.** Maybe you are near retirement. Maybe you have health issues. Maybe you are tired of all the attention your rental property requires. Owning rental property can be very profitable, but no one will claim that it comes without work. If the property no longer fits your plans, maybe it's time to cash in your chips.

5) **You're in a good situation with capital gains tax.** If you're not sure if you are in a good situation regarding capital gains tax, you should consult with your financial advisor. If you're able to sell your property without a lot of capital gains taxes, you're in a good position to sell.

Five Crucial Exit Strategies for Your Real Estate Investments

What's an exit strategy, you ask? Simply, it is an investment property owner's plan to remove himself or herself from an investment. Many successful real estate investors will have a specific exit plan in place when they enter into an investment. Others will wait to get into the investment and see how it is going and then develop their exit plans. Either way, it's important to develop some kind of exit plan early on in the process, so you can quickly determine when to exit the investment. Investors who don't have exit plans will often hold on to properties too long, possibly costing them thousands of dollars (sometimes ten thousands or hundred thousands of dollars).

Investors will exit properties for a number of reasons. Maybe the time is right to make a max profit on the property. Maybe they want to exit the property and use the profits to purchase higher level properties or investments. Maybe the investor has determined that real property investment just isn't for them. Maybe the investor is retiring or has health problems or a family or financial emergency.

Here are five main exit strategies for real estate investors:

1) **Fix and flip.** Although this strategy doesn't have anything to do with rental property, it deserves mention as a real estate property exit strategy because of the popularity of flipping, in which investors will purchase properties, work quickly to upgrade those properties, and then sell them for a profit.

Rental Properties

2) **Buy and hold.** This strategy has everything to do with rental property investment, as buyers will buy property, sometimes renovate it/sometimes not, and then they will lease the property to renters with the idea of making steady cash flow from the property as they build equity. Hopefully for the investor, the property will appreciate in value at the same time it creates steady cash flow and then the buyer can sell the property at the appropriate time and turn a nice profit.

3) **Wholesaling.** This is when someone acts as a middleman in a property purchase. They will purchase the property without any intention of occupying the property or rehabbing the property, and then they will turn around and sell it for a profit to an end buyer. This exit strategy is somewhat similar to a fix and flip strategy, however the wholesaler doesn't put any sweat equity into the project (no rehabbing or renovation). Unlike flipping, which can bring huge profits if done correctly, wholesaling generally brings lower profit margins.

4) **Seller financing.** With this strategy, the seller acts as a bank. In essence, the seller finances the purchase of the property, with the seller and the buyer having a promissory note that includes the agreed-upon interest rate and a payment schedule. From a seller standpoint, the seller gets to continue to derive income from the property to cover the mortgage loan and their return on investment also increases due to the interest rate.

5) **Rent to own.** With this exit strategy, the property owner will rent the investment property to a tenant, and then after a pre-determined/set period of time, the tenant will be able to purchase the property from the seller. In some cases in a rent to own agreement, a portion of the monthly rental payment will be set aside toward the purchase of the home. This type of agreement allows the seller to

Rental Properties

continue to derive income from the property and then if the tenant/potential buyer walks away from the property for whatever reason, the seller has still continued to establish equity in the property.

It should be pointed out that there are numerous factors that will determine whether an investor should exit a property. Long-term goals versus short-term goals will often be a factor. Purchase price of the property, value of the property, and condition of the property may also be factors. Supply and demand, profit potential, market conditions, and financing options will also be factors.

Even if an investor has an exit plan at the outset of purchasing a property, those plans can be derailed by numerous factors. If the property depreciates, the investor may want to dump sooner than expected or make wait until the property rebounds. Tenant issues might escalate or delay the sale of a property. The same goes for unexpected major maintenance costs. Poor property management can have a major impact on the profitability of a property and when that property will be sold. And finally, a distinct lack of demand can affect the exit strategy for a property. You can't sell a property for which there's no demand.

Conclusion

Well, if you've read this far, you should now know a lot more than when you started about the opportunities that are available for you in real estate property rentals. You should have a better understanding of what real estate rental investments can do for you and how you can make money from those investments. You'll know that if you can pay attention to all the areas and responsibilities of real estate rental property investment, you'll have a chance to make money, sometimes a lot of money. You'll also know that if you neglect any areas of real estate rental property investment, you'll inhibit your chances for success and possibly even fail.

You now know how to evaluate properties for possible investment and you also know how to evaluate the neighborhoods or areas those properties are in. You know all about the 1% Rule and the formula for making sure that the properties you are investing in are viable. As many of you are first-time investors, you're going to have to determine ways to finance your first property, often times without a lot of available cash. We've told you about house hacking, a great way to break into the real estate rental property business. We also given you other ideas on how to get properties with no money down and other techniques on how to save money you can use for the down payment toward your property.

We've touched briefly on commercial real estate rental property investment, which is generally for investors as they move up the food chain from novice to expert. We told you to "draft" and develop a real estate team to ensure your success as an investor and we've told you who to include on that team.

Rehabbing properties is extremely important with most Class C and some Class B rental properties. We've given you a step-by-step guide on how rehab properties. Along the same lines, you now know what kind of rehab projects are most important for rental properties. And you also know some simple and inexpensive rehab projects you can do to increase the value of the property immediately.

As a landlord, you'll have to decide how you want to manage your property. Will you want to use the hands-on approach, the mixed approach, or the outsource approach? Regardless of which approach you choose, you'll have to do everything possible to secure good tenants for your property. Good tenants can be the lifeblood of any rental property investments; bad tenants can break you.

As most people get into real estate rental to make money, you'll find that you'll be well served if you have an exit plan for the properties you invest in. "Know when to fold 'em", as Kenny Rogers would say. We've outlined the main reasons people exit properties and also the strategies they use in exiting those properties.

In conclusion, owning real estate rental property can be very lucrative financially, if you can focus on all the different areas of the business. If you can do the research to find good properties at a good price, if you can find good tenants and take care of those tenants, if you can manage the properties well, you'll have a great chance to be successful. That being said, owner rental property in not a hobby. It's not easy money; you'll have to pay attention to detail if you're going to succeed. But if you'll utilize many of the tips and techniques offered in this book, you're likely to be successful and well on the way to financial freedom.

With that said, we'll leave you with six words: Wishing you success! Let's get after it!

The Secrets of Successful House Flipping

Do You Have an Eye for Spotting Real Estate Investing Opportunities? Discover How to Make Big Bucks Flipping Houses without a Large Initial Investment

Table of Contents

Introduction **101**

Chapter 1 – House-Flipping Fundamentals **107**

    What Does 'Flipping Houses' Mean? 107

    Build a House-Flipping Mindset that Paves the Way for Success 110

    The 8 Steps to Flipping a House 115

Chapter 2 - Understanding the Market **122**

    How to Properly Research & Analyze Your Local Real Estate Market 122

    Following the 70% Rule 127

    Is it a Buyer's, Seller's, or Balanced Market? 131

Chapter 3 - No Money, No Problem **136**

    Wholesaling: All You Need to Know to Get Started 136

    How to Get a Hard Money Loan 140

    Flipping Houses With No Money Using Private Investors 144

Chapter 4 - Choosing the Right Property **148**

    Key Factors For Choosing The Right Location 148

    Features to Look For & Features to Avoid in Property 153

    Golden Rules for Picking Property 158

    How to Calculate Your Net Profit 162

Chapter 5 - It's All About Value **165**

    The 4 Best Value-Boosting Renovations 165

    Curb Appeal: What It Is & How to Do It Right 171

    Small Updates for a Significantly More Desirable Home 174

    Green Improvements that Instantly Increase a Home's Value 177

Chapter 6 - Making It Shine 179
Putting Together The Rehab Dream Team 179
How to Find the Best Contractor for Your Property 185

Make It Shine While Minimizing Costs 189

Chapter 7 - Completing the Flip 194
The Lowdown on Selling Your Property Yourself vs. Through a Realtor 194

5 Best Marketing Strategies for Real Estate 197

How to Stage Your Property to Win Over Buyers 201

Chapter 8 - Staying Smart 206
House-flipping mistakes to avoid at all costs 206
4 warning signs your house-flip is flopping 210

4 exit strategies to always keep in mind 213

CONCLUSION – THE TAKEAWAYS 219

Flipping Houses

Introduction

Has your cousin Jerry bragged about how he converted a $50K teardown into a $250K house? Do you have an eye for decaying properties on your commute to work and think to yourself "I could fix that up and sell that"? Do you fantasize about converting old abandoned shacks into livable, gorgeous homes until you become a real estate millionaire like Donald Trump? Maybe your hobby is to analyze real estate properties on the internet and you've accumulated knowledge about the real estate market in your area, enough that you're on the brink of getting into house flipping. House-flipping is the best way you to get your foot in real estate! It is the art of identifying future potential, investing in it and re-selling for a profit.

The average person looks at a house in bad shape and thinks: "That house is ugly". A house-flipper looks at a house in bad shape and thinks: "That house is my next paycheck!". A house-flipper is no different than an entrepreneur on Wall Street who invests in stocks: They identify a stock with future potential, invest their capital in it and cash out when the value increases. The difference is that house-flipping doesn't require luck and a house flippers can artificially raise the value of a property in as little as a few weeks with adequate repairs and renovations. This book will prepare you for the experience of a house-flipper by showing you the big secrets and the step-by-step to prepare you for your new life as a house flipper. The book will give you a kick in the butt and that last "push" you need if you're on the fence about house-flipping. It will give you all the details you need to reassure you and prepare you for your first flip.

We're here to hand it to you: The insider knowledge for all levels of investment - whether you're starting off broke or a millionaire, there are investments for every level obtainable. We'll explain which properties are investing in, so you don't waste your time on low-return properties with no potential. Just because the properties are cheap, doesn't mean they're going to give you returns. Don't worry, we'll tell you exactly where to look: Which states, the classification of neighborhoods, the types of properties that sell, the building permits, the zoning laws, the regulations, the contractors and finally how to sell your properties. We cover in great detail how to locate rare valuable properties, how to renovate, how to hire affordable contractors, cover legal fees and ultimately sell your property for the equivalent of a yearly salary.

1# Secret To House-Flipping

But before we start... Here's one secret you've never been told about house flipping:

- You don't have to be a millionaire!

That's right, you don't have to be a millionaire to get your foot in the door with house-flipping. You merely have to be a thousandnaire! We teach you numerous ways to acquire capital for your first property and how to present your investment as "low risk" to financiers who will bankroll your first flip. The key here is that there are investments for all income levels: If you have millions to spend, we'll teach you how to source-out high-value properties in class-A neighborhoods that you can flip for millions. If you have immediate access to capital, you can start flipping without consulting any financial institutions.

The US median home value is currently $230,000. That means that it's possible to find houses or condos for less than $230,000 and in many cases less than $100,000 that are still inhabitable. The mortgage on a $100,000 house can be as low as $400/month and the average down-payment is a mere 20%. Let's say you have no money to invest at all but you want to get into house-flipping. How easy would it be for you to accumulate $20,000 for a down-payment, fix up the house and flip it for a profit in 6 months? As you see, the barrier of entry is a lot lower than people imagine. If you have a 9-5 job and you save up for a year, there is a high chance you will be able to afford a down-payment. Once you've successfully flipped your first property, you can quit your job and get into house-flipping full-time – to become your own boss.

Pro Tip: The property you "flip" does not have to stand out, it just has to be livable. We encourage novices to start off by flipping average, working-class homes. Go for a drive in your city and observe the houses for 30 minutes. What do you notice? Average house. Average house. Average house. Over 90% of the real estate market is comprised up of average dwellings. Why focus on that one multi-million dollar home, when the middle-income market constitutes almost the entire market? Take a look at what constitutes the majority of your city. It's always going to be regular houses. This is where the money's at! Regular people need a place to live - your job is to provide them a home. Think: The retired veteran's property from across the street. Take your middle school's buddy house and flip that. A property doesn't have to be ran down to be flipped, it can be regular livable house which you upgrade by making small improvements.

The focus in this book is on dwellings for the average person will reside in and we make it our goal to identify multiple "flippable" properties until we start seeing consecutive ROI on our investments. If you focus on house-building and make it your #1 business, you are almost guaranteed to become a millionaire over the course of your lifetime. We focus on safe properties in high-growth areas that sell fast. You won't get rich in your first year, but you will immediately make enough money to pay the bills and finance much bigger deals. Moreover, if you flip one house that is a sign you can definitely flip another 10. Once you've flipped 10 houses, you can flip an entire neighborhood. Once you flipped a neighborhood, you can move on to buildings and commercial properties. Once you get into buildings and commercial properties, the sky is the limit! We explain the safest, idiot-proof house-flipping methods that beginners with little/no investment capital can use to capitalize on the housing market.

#2 Secret To House-Flipping

Here's the second secret about house-flipping:

- You don't have to know "trades" to fix houses!

If you think you need to know about plumbing, painting, wiring and roofing to flip a house, you couldn't be more wrong. Your job as a house-flipper is to do the administrative tasks: To identify properties with high potential, to convince financiers to put up the initial money, to hire contractors who fix the property and ultimately flip the house. You don't need to know the first thing about roof shingles and/or Persian rugs, you hire people to do that for you. In essence, you must be the person who "brings it all together". You're the missing link between all those contractors, bankers and buyers. Your job is to ensure everyone sees a return on their investment, which ultimately provides you with a return on your investment. Your job is to persuade the investors, to sign off the checks for the blue-collar workers and provide buyers with an adequate livable space in which they can reside. This book will prepare you for each step of the way.

#3 Secret To House-Flipping

Here's the third secret about house-flipping:

- The market itself will increase the value of your property!

On average, the yearly median home value in the US increases by 3-6%. Example: If you purchased a house for $300,000 in 3 years it would be worth between $330,000 and $360,000. That is $30,000-60,000 increase in value while doing absolutely nothing! If you sat on it for a decade that same property would be worth at least $400,000. That's $100,000 in the bank, and don't forget you still own the place. House-flippers obsess over "fixing up" the house in order to solidify its value. Bear in mind livable houses will always increase in value as the economy goes up - one can sit and down nothing and the value of the property will increase in as little as a few years.

How many people do you know who bought a property for $50,000 in 1980 and that same property is now worth $1,5M? The increase in value is through the roof. The only question that remains: How do you predict which areas are going to gentrify over the next 5-10 years? How do you analyze the type of neighborhoods that are worth investing in and will remain wealthy? In this book we focus on areas that sell immediately and help you identify the hottest markets in the US. This way your first property will not remain on the market for longer than a week - you'll have people calling you and begging to give you their money.

#4 Secret To House Flipping

The fourth and final secret to house-flipping:

- *You can flip your first house in 3 months!*

House-flipping is not an infinite process where you wait for a year before you can sell a house. You can flip a house in as little as 12 weeks! All you have to do is purchase is investigate the market, purchase a property, fix it up and sell it. We explain how to do each step in great detail in the book. Many of you will have different levels of knowledge about house-flipping. If you have no idea what it stands for, pay extra attention in the first chapters. The speed and efficiency will depend on your capital: If you have capital to invest immediately, you can flip a house in as little as a four weeks. This is because you can finance the house and repairs immediately, while someone without immediate access to capital will have to wait for approval and plan out their investments months in advance. In both cases the same principles and methods listed in this book apply!

How To Navigate This Book

We lay out the basics for beginners: If you don't know where to start, the terminology, what mindset you need to obtain to be successful in house-flipping, how to finance your first house and the neighborhoods to invest in, focus on the introductory chapters. If you have a more advanced level of knowledge and you wish to learn more about how to lower your costs for contractors and which houses sell in the current market and how to finance bigger deals – move straight to the advanced chapters.

Chapter 1 – House-Flipping Fundamentals

What Does 'Flipping Houses' Mean?

You're about to become a house-flipper - congratulations! You're about to experience the glamour of the "Sold!" sign on your first house flip, and you are a few months away from handing the keys of your first flip to your first client. You are in for a journey: You're about to see your investments materialize and a big, fat check to compensate you for all your hard work. The key to real-estate riches and making the right moves is to be diligent about details. That has everything to do with your property purchases, the expenses you accumulate and putting your home on the market. We'll teach you step-by-step how to minimize your initial expenses on your first purchase, how to minimize your expenses on the upgrades and finally make the average US salary on every single flip. This is our end goal for everyone reading this!

House-Flipping: The Definition

Important: House-flipping is not about taking houses and turning them upside down! It's about buying a house as an investment, improving it and selling it for a profit. "House Flipping" is sometimes referred to as "wholesale real estate investing" and it's a real-estate investment strategy in which you purchase a property with the intention of re-selling it instead of settling down in it yourself.

You've seen many successful, well-dressed real-estate millionaires flipping houses on TV and sharing their experience with the world. You want to emulate them and become a success story, or maybe you

Flipping Houses

want to flip a house to add to your existing income. Three are more than 200,000 houses being bought, fixed and re-sold in the United States each year. If you could only fix up 10 house a year, you would be a millionaire in as little as a few years. Does this sound incentivizing? There are people in the US currently flipping 5 new houses a week and remodeling them. The hardest "flip" is usually your very first flip: You don't know what to expect, how much contractors will charge you, you don't know how permits work and you don't know how to buy/sell a property. Worry not, this guide has the nitty-gritty details you need to give you the confidence for each step. Pay close attention as this might change your life.

How House Flipping Works

To be successful in house flipping, there are usually two ways in which investors use to make a profit: 1) From appreciation in a "hot" real estate market or 2) Capital investments in a property which increase its value. Most house-flippers choose the latter and purchase an average property and equip it with state-of-the-art amenities such as a new floor, paint, kitchen, and bathroom. If a property costs $100,000 and the upgrades cost $40,000, the investor can easily sell that home for $200,000. The "strategy" for flipping is identical to other investment principles: buying low and selling high. Time is of the essence in house-flipping the costs increase the longer a flipper has to pay for insurance and property taxes rise, hence the average "flip" takes 6 months. Established flippers might purchase 5-10 new properties each week.

But stop! Before we reveal the insider secrets of house flipping, before we teach you the mindsets that are conducive to a successful flip, and before we tell you how to purchase properties for below market-value - we must teach you the very basics of house-flipping and what they entail.

House-Flipping Basics: ARV ("After Repair Value")

Pro Tip: The most important term in house-flipping is "ARV" - "After Repair Value". If you plan to sell a home for $250,000, your RAV for that home is $250,000. Once the home is remodeled, spanking-shiny and ready to be listed on the market – this is the ARV (the final selling price on the market). Remember the term ARV as it refers to the final value of the home once repairs are carried out. The ARV formula is simple to understand: Original home value + Repair costs = ARV (after repair value).

House-flipping revolves around ARV as all calculations stem from the final investment value which the investor plans to invest into the property. Remember what the acronym ARV stands for as you'll be hearing that very often in this book, and among your house-flipping crowd. ARV determines the repairs and upgrades you'll have to make to a property before you're prepared to list it on the market. What are the rules of ARV and how to calculate expenses?

House-Flipping Basics: The 70% Rule Of ARV

The 70% rule is the most famous rule-of-thumb in house-flipping. This rule helps to calculate the expenses on a home before you even put down a payment on a property. The 70% rule commands that a house-flipper should not pay more than 70% of the total ARV (after repair value) minus the repair costs involved. This gives leeway for a house-flipper to make at least 30% profit on each sale. In some cases the profit can be as much as 40%, however, as a rule of thumb - investors stick to a safe 30%. Remember that ARV is not just the initial costs and the repairs, but it's the final value of the property.

The 70% Rule:

➔ **(ARV x 0.70) – Repair Costs = X (maximum amount you should spend on a property).**

Pro Tip: Take your calculator and calculate the first house-flip you'll make. For the examples below, we'll take two houses - one with a value of $200,000 that requires $40,000 in repairs and another with a value of $150,000 that requires $30,000 in repairs.

Example #1: $200,000 x 0.70 - $40,000 = $100,000.

Example #2: $150,000 x 0.70 - $30,000 = $75,000

In total, the investor should NOT exceed spending of $100,000 for the acquisition of the first property in order to close a $200,000 sale at the end. For the second house, the investor should NOT spend more than $75,000 on a house in order to sell it for $150,000.

The 70% rule is important because each house is different and requires a different set of repairs. Some houses might be worth $200,000 and require only $20,000 in repairs while other houses of the same value would require $50,000 in repairs. The ARV is the most important calculation you'll have to make in house-flipping in order to determine your profitability at the end. The 70% rule provides a "buffer" in case of unexpected expenses on your first flip which would increase the cost of repairs and prevent you from making a profit.

Ran your first calculation? Congrats, you're 50% of the way to becoming a house-flipper! Now that you know how to calculate your expenses in advance, we'll get into the success mindset you need to obtain and cover each step of the investment process in detail.

Build a House-Flipping Mindset that Paves the Way for Success

House-flipping requires mental shifts that are conducive to being effective in the business in general. A house-flipper can't think like an average person – a house-flipper must think 6 months in advance and have the know-how to calibrate to construction problems once they arise. The challenge of house-flipping is to prepare for the finish line before you even start and learn how to deal with problems as they arise, without losing sight of the big picture. The key principles of house-flipping are the following 5 principles: 1) Preparation, 2) efficiency, 3) decisiveness, 4) action-taking and 5) patience. The way those principles apply to the day-to-day of house flipping are in the mindsets which you will learn below. These principles and mind-shifts are conductive to a house-flipper who wishes to execute their flip in the most efficient way possible:

Top 5 Principles Of House-Flipping

1) Preparation

The average house-flip takes 6 months from purchase to sale. On average, you'll have to spend a month researching a property, gathering documents, hiring lawyers, preparing the finances and signing off the checks. This process can be lengthy, especially on wholesale purchases such as foreclosed properties. Once you've purchased the property, you'll have to hire individual contractors for each step of the way. If the rooms need painting, you'll have to source out painting contractors. If you need the wires changed, you'll have to source out electricians. All of them bid their unique price and you must estimate the cost of each repair before you purchase the property. Once you're fully prepared, you can make the purchase and start fixing the property until it's done. Preparation work is the most crucial process for ensuring you make a profit at the end.

2) Efficiency

The way you execute each process will determine the final sale price of the property. Did you hire poor contractors who messed up the tiles on the floor? This can take away from the impression clients have on the property and lower your sale price. As a property developer, you must care for each detail and apply diligence to make sure the small repairs you make will match the big picture of the home.

Example: It's safer to paint each room in a single white color than paint each room individually. In areas that are out of your control such as hiring contractors - you must be efficient in choosing the best contractors possible.

3) Decisiveness

House-flipping is not like on TV! The real day-to-day of house-flipping is messy. Many times you will run into problems you never expected which can increase the costs of your repairs.

Example: You might discover molding on the roof that requires you to change the entire roof. You might be faced with a roach infestation in the bathroom. Despite the fact that you carried out a thorough investigation upon purchase, you will still experience hurdles along the way. Prepare for this by being decisive! Don't dwell on complex solutions but focus on the simplest solution you can find. In most cases the solutions to big problems are simple. If the roof needs replacing, allocate a higher percentage of your budget on the roof - this is more essential than picking out fancy tiles for the bathroom. Make the call!

4) Action-Taking

Remember: Action cures fear! Action-taking will remove the paranoia you have about things going wrong or your investment going down the drain. Once you're actually in the thick of your repairs, you will start enjoying them and you'll find house-flipping fun. You're creating value for society on many levels: You're providing liquidity for people who you bought the house from in the first place. You're giving jobs to contractors who feed their families on your repairs. You're doing a service to the future owners of the property by providing them a home. Remind yourself of that every time you doubt yourself and go to work!

5) Patience

Most houses are flipped within 6-12 months. Want to do it in 1 month? It's possible but you will likely have to work around the clock and have connections with contractors who can help you immediately. Most quality contractors are booked months in advance and you will have to be patient in terms of legal permits which can take weeks or months depending on the state/municipality. Patience is crucial when you the property is fixed too - it might sit on the market for longer than you expect unless it's in a "hot" market. Be patient because this is not something you'll accomplish overnight. Prepare for at least half a year on your first flip. Once you've done that, try to cut the time on your next flip by half. Build up efficiency gradually.

Top 3 Mind-Shifts For House Flipping

The principles of house-flipping apply to all areas of success - there are also specific mind-shifts which apply only to house-flipping. Use the mind-shifts below to ensure you end up successful in your house-flipping endeavors:

Mind-shift #1: Focus On Speed

Limit the amount of time you take to complete all transactions: Buying, fixing and selling. The key mind-shift you must make it to focus on speed in the short-term and have patience in the long-term. How do you align the two? You must have faith that no matter how long the flip takes, you will be able to pull it off. However, you must accelerate your day-to-day in order to speed up the process of gathering finances, hiring contractors, legalizing the building and selling the fixed property. Your sole focus on your day-to-day should be on speed instead of maximizing profit. Each day your property sits on the market will end up costing you more and this is why accelerating the process is crucial. If you can flip the whole property within 1 month, do it! There is no "rule" saying the property has to sit on the market for 6 months. Always cut down the time in half: If you think a flip is going to take a year, try to do it in 6 months!

REMEMBER: The longer you hold on to a property, the more you're risking your finances. Many things can go wrong with the property if you hold it for months: It could be burglarized, destroyed in a hurricane, the quality of repairs deteriorates, etc. There are also added costs which you must account for before purchase: The utilities, mortgage payment, insurance payments, property taxes, and more. Example of hidden-costs: Insurance for house-flips will cost 2x regular home insurance because you must purchase "vacancy insurance" for the home.

Mind-shift #2: Cheap Is Not Always Profitable

Don't rush to buy a house! There are many reasons why a property is cheap: It can be a sketchy neighborhood, no access to infrastructure, or back taxes owed on the property. Do you remember headlines of houses going for $10 or even $1 in Detroit? Those same houses can have $10,000 or even $20,000 in back-taxes owed by the previous owners that weren't paid for decades. The new owner will have to pay those taxes out of pocket. If the neighborhood doesn't have access to good schools, families will be reluctant to purchase your property. We explain how to shift neighborhood classifications and identify thriving neighborhoods where you can purchase properties on the cheap.

Mind-shift #3: Overestimate Your Initial Costs

Things can always go wrong in house-flipping. Do you think because you bought in a rich area that your property is safe? You could purchase a home in a safe, wealthy, educated district and the contractors could ruin everything. Many times flippers end up barely making their money back or even losing money on their first flip. This is due to overhead on expenses they didn't prepare for in advance.

Example: Let's say you can paint. You need to paint 3 rooms in the house and you think it would take you 5 hours to paint each room. If you seek out contractors who work for $30/h, that would mean they would charge you $150 per room. However, many of them will bid $300-500 per room. Why does that happen? You might over-estimate how fast you can paint each room yourself. The contractors might need more time, or they have overhead, or maybe they're even plain greedy! Always expect to spend more than you initially calculate or consult multiple contractors for a bid until you can decisively conclude the average cost of each repair.

Once you've internalized the aforementioned principles and mind-shifts, you're ready for the war of house-flipping! Bring it on!

The 8 Steps to Flipping a House

It's time to pull up your sleeves and do the dirty work! Excited? Let's get the ball rolling. House-flipping is not like in the TV shows. You don't magically purchase a house, renovate it in the snap of a finger and $50,000 magically appears in your bank account. You must do due-diligence research of neighborhoods, finance the purchase, follow zoning laws, carry out renovations and ultimately sell the property.

Pro Tip: House-flipping is "messy" in real life. You will never sell a property the way you imagined to, and each property will require individual attention and care. One property might work smooth and fast, and another property might become a nightmare to renovate. The guidelines below are only to give you an idea as to what to expect. Moreover, there is no "ultimate" way to house-flip. You must find your ideal method yourself! Let's say you refuse to hire realtors and sell the property yourself (to keep their 5% commission). There is no written law that you must use a realtor! You might also refuse to hire contractors and bring a family member to do the renovations yourself. It's up to you to discover what works for you.

The top 6 steps to house-flipping will help get you get your foot in the world of house-flipping. The steps we present will help you become a professional on your first flip - avoiding the mistakes that novices make. For example, many novices rush to purchase their first property and don't carry out inspections which end up costing them more than their profit. If you follow our steps, you will know which houses to buy and use an inspector who will verify the house is in good shape for renovations. We also teach you which renovations to carry out and which ones to skip. Advance stages such as the capital gains tax and zoning laws will be explained further, but if you follow the 6-steps you will be successful on your first flip:

1) Network With Real Estate Experts

New to house-flipping? Forget about the house! Forget about banks and renovations. Start by talking to actual house-flippers in your area. Visit an event for real estate and network with people who flip houses for a living. This will be crucial as they have connections to all the contractors you'll need: electricians, roofers, plumbers, general contractors, painters, HVAC people, handymen, etc. You will eventually need the assistance of some of those people. In general, one could look up "x area + contractor" to find a local contractor, but if you know house-flippers who have used those contractors before it will make your job a lot easier.

Warning: Many times a contractor will promise you "We'll get it done in 1 week" and a month later they're still playing with the drywall. You need to get in touch with verified contractors who carry out work efficiently. The best way to do this is to consult people who are like you, before you even attempt your first flip. In most cases those people will also have "insider" information as to bureaucracy and flipping secrets that you would only discover after years in the business.

How do you source out real estate people? Won't they see you as competition? We hear you, but the answer is simple - pay them. If you contact a flipper or an established real estate firm (both of which work in construction and hire the same contractors), you can offer to pay them $1000 to have them "on call" once you run into problems and need access to information about contractors. This is a small price to pay for access to the best contractors in your area. You're making them an "offer they can't refuse" because they know they have to do minimal work and it's more likely to work than demanding their connections empty-handed.

2) Research Neighborhoods

In real estate there are "classes" based on the gentrification level of a neighborhood. There are only 4 classes: A, B, C and D. A-class neighborhoods are the "elite" neighborhoods in a city. Class-A's are populated by the most affluent individuals, celebrities, politicians, and the general upper echelon of society. The expense of a house in a Class-A neighborhood will depend on the city. In more affluent cities, the average going price for a home could be $1M. In less wealthier cities, a Class-A neighborhoods might have an average price of $500,000.

Class-A flips are the safest as the houses are always in demand and they have the best access to infrastructure, schools and safety. Class-B neighborhoods are "upper middle income" neighborhoods: The most typical representation of the "American Dream". Class-B houses can be quite sizable. Class-C neighborhoods are considered "working class" neighborhoods, and are usually populated by middle-income residents. Class-D neighborhoods are low-income neighborhoods and properties there cost less.

What are the best neighborhoods? It depends - the cheapest class-D neighborhoods might have many "great deals" but insurance premiums are higher as the risk of crime and home invasions increases. Class-A neighborhoods are mostly out of reach for novice flippers. Most novice flippers start with Class-C or Class-B neighborhoods.

Pro Tip: Your flip is not confined to neighborhood research. You could technically purchase a rural, isolated property and flip that property. Neighborhood classification is merely an economic indicator for the prosperity of a neighborhood.

3) Calculate Total Budget

It's time to bust out your calculator! Calculate your budget, how much you can afford on the property and how much will go on renovations. This is not hard - it's common sense! Let's say you only have $20,000 to set aside for repairs, in that case you should stay away from $500,000 houses. The ideal flip for you would be a house in the sub $100,000< range. If you have $200,000 to spare on renovations, you should consider getting into class-A houses estimated at $500,000-1M. As a rule of thumb, estimate that the down-payment on the house will be 20%. In this case, there are clear differences between a down-payment on a $500,000 house and down-payment on a $50,000 house. Calculate how much you can spend on the house pre-renovations.

Once you've calculated the down-payment and total cost of acquisition, you must factor in the renovation expenses. The sale price should never exceed the price of acquisition, renovation and maintenance (utilities, property taxes, insurance, etc). Let's say you add a $15,000 kitchen, $10,000 bathroom, $5000 in yearly maintenance costs and other carrying costs - add the highest expenses you expect and combine that with the acquisition cost. Now add an unexpected structural problem to stay safe. Don't forget that even after you sell, the average gross profit on a flip in the United States is $60,000. Once capital gains taxes set in, it's even less. The lower your renovation costs, the more money in your pocket at the end of the flip!

4) Finance The Purchase

It's time to take out the liquid for the purchase - you must prepare money before you start visiting houses, talking to real-estate owners or realtors. If you have access to capital you can skip this part entirely and focus on the acquisition! However, if you don't you must secure the funds yourself. The good news: You don't have access to 6-figure sums, there are many workarounds that will supply you the capital you need. Most people either opt for bank lending or they rely on private lending. We cover how to secure a bank loan or consult private lenders who will finance the whole purchase for a cut at the final flip price.

Once you've secured funding, that's when the fun starts. Keep in mind you're paying interest from day 1. The bank interest on borrowed money for a property is tax-deductible, and despite cuts in the Jobs Act, the interest is not a 100% cut. Once you add in the principal, capital gains taxes and double rates for vacancy insurance, none of those are deductible.

This is the right time to consult an accountant or a lawyer - those professionals will estimate the total cost for all legal/tax expenses and allow you to estimate the cost on the flip, renovations and hidden-charges. This will reassure you that the purchase you're making is a safe one.

5) Investigate The Property

Secured the money? Ready to get the keys? Wait, don't rush to buy that house yet! New house-flippers rush this and a month later they discover a structural problem that eats up their entire renovation budget. Send them a home inspector first. A home inspector is a professional who can be sent on-location to investigate the entire property for any kind of structural problem. They will give you a detailed report as to the state of the property, the renovations necessary and the total expenses for all the repairs needed.

Home inspectors are imperative to ensuring the property you're about to purchase is structural sound and that the internal infrastructural and mechanical systems are functional. Once the inspector verifies you won't run into "unpleasant surprises", you can start signing checks and shaking hands.

6) Acquire The Property

The exciting stuff! Once you've investigated a property, it's time to get the keys to the house. This property will now belong to you and it becomes your responsibility. There are many ways to purchase a property. Most flippers purchase directly from sellers to avoid agent fees. To find the best "deals" you might purchase foreclosed properties where the owner failed to make a payment or a tragic accident happened such as death, divorce or financial distress. It's not "immoral" to purchase from these people, as you're providing liquidity that will help them start a new life. No matter how you purchase the property, you will have to sign off legal papers and get the procedure notarized. Consider hiring a lawyer for the process, to verify there are no "loopholes" and that you actually own the property. If something looks fishy, refuse to sign. Let your lawyer have a detailed look at every paper and then put your signature on it.

IMPORTANT: You must prepare for inspections that the municipality will send out after you buy a property. The local municipality will send inspectors who will consult with you and "investigate" your property to ensure it follows municipal building codes. Inspections will be rigid in most "prime" neighborhoods that maintain high standards. Virtually all municipalities will send inspections before you're allowed to sell a property. If the investigators detect something is wrong with the property you will have to spend more time and money fixing it until it meets their standards.

7) Renovate The Property

You have the keys to the house – what now? You must renovate it to increase its value. This is where the "sweat equity" kicks in, the stuff they don't show on TV. This is also when ugly surprises come up. What if you find out the bathroom is infested with roaches at night? You could never guess that even with an inspector. You will have to hire contactors to exterminate the infestation - the same with rats, ants or any rodents on the property. Is the paint bad in one room? You'll have to paint every room to make sure that doesn't stand out. You must calibrate to the needs of each individual property. This is when you'll need assistance from your real-estate friends who can put you in touch with contractors: electricians, plumbers, carpenters, roofers, gardeners, etc. Even if you execute everything perfectly there is no guarantee your contractors won't mess up! If they tell you they'll get it done in 2 days, they might discover the job is harder and requires a week of repairs. Expect delays and increased charges.

Pro Tip: To make more money you must spend less on renovations. How do you pull that off? Learn to "fix" things yourself. If you're handy with a hammer, if you can install a kitchen sink, if you know how to roof or hang drywall - you have skills that will save you thousands of dollars off the bat. If you can't work with equipment, lack the skills or outright don't want to get your hands dirty - there are always professionals who will deploy to your location and get the job done.

8) Sell The Property

This is the final part - the part where you see 5 or 6 digit amounts hit your bank account! There are ways to save money on the sale too! If you don't know any trades but you like selling, you can sell your own property directly. There are many ways to sell a property online which we'll explain further. If you turn to a real-estate agency they will offer to sell your property for 5% commission and the lowest they'll go is 4%. This is a hefty sum to pay on your first property. Why give it away when you can sell the property yourself? We'll explain how to tap into the "for sale by owner" market and sell your property within a matter of weeks.

Chapter 2 - Understanding the Market

How to Properly Research & Analyze Your Local Real Estate Market

You stumbled upon a great deal in suburban New Jersey: A $90,000 house with access to schools, hospitals and good infrastructure. How do you analyze if the $90,000 price is adequate for that location, square footage and structural shape? Analyzing the immediate area of your property will help you determine the average price of a house. Don't make the call yet: It's time to search for previous "Sold" properties in the area that will give you comparable properties to know if you're getting a good deal or being ripped off! Those properties are called "comps" in the real estate industry - identical properties with identical square footage (that sold in your area recently). Comps are only viable if they sold in the last 6 months. If a property sold a year ago, it doesn't tell you much about the current state of the market. This is why accumulating recent data is essential for comps, and then cross-referencing the data with an appraiser who can estimate the home value based on the maintenance level and structural integrity.

To discover comps for your property, you must analyze properties within a 1/2 mile range of your property that sold within the last 3-6 months. Each property you stumble upon that sold can be classified as a "comp". However, you must seek out properties with similar or identical square footage to determine the average price. There are tools that can help you narrow down your research such as Zillow and Redfin that provide "estimates" as to the average house value in each zip code and can vaguely estimate the price of a house using mapping data. However, to get accurate real-world data you have to analyze properties that were actually sold as estimates can be completely off-base.

What happens if it's impossible to discover properties that sold of similar square footage? To get around a shortage of "sold" properties, you must analyze other properties that are larger or smaller that can give you a value comparison, and estimate by doing the math on the difference.

Example: You have your $90,000 property in NJ and the property is 2000 sq ft. If you discover a larger property such as one of 2500 sq ft. that sold in the area for the same price, you might be getting a bad deal. However, if you find similar prices for sold properties then this is potentially a good deal. At the end, it's important to cross-reference your comps with a local realtor and/or appraiser who can estimate the value of a property and indicators that might increase or decrease property value such as proximity to amenities, healthcare/educational institutions and general shape of the property. Realtors deal with local real estate markets, making them more effective at determining local home value.

Pro Tip: Realtors can help you estimate the sale price on your house flip in advance. Once you've gathered a list of comps, you will have access to data for the average listing price for a home of that square footage in your area. You can then consult a realtor to help you with the final calculations. The realtor will help you identify the most accurate comps, analyze the property you're trying to acquire and calculate the final potential price for based on the condition of the property.

4 Steps Of Using Comps To Determine Home Value

Once you've found a suitable property, it's time to gather your list of "comps"! Not all properties that sold in your area are eligible. The "comps" are only homes that sold in recent time (3-6 months) and have similar features to your home. Before you put down a payment on a house, you must analyze comps and identify which one is the closest to your future property. You must either use online tools that enable you to research properties in your area using maps, or Google "Neighborhood + sold properties" to discover realtors who sold properties in your area and find out if they sold a property of similar square footage. The following 4 steps will help you identify comps for your future property:

Step #1) Identify Properties In 1/2 Mile Radius

Location, location, location! The properties have to be in the same neighborhood or within a short 1/2 mile radius to qualify as comps. Home value can increase and decrease within a single mile because certain areas are blocked off from major roads or have terrain difficulties that cut them off from receiving infrastructure that reflect in the listing price. Find a list of all the closest properties that sold recently and calculate the average value based on the information. Don't look at listings for sale, but focus on properties that sold already. This will give you an accurate estimate as to the average price per square foot. If a comp is too far from your property, it might give you the wrong idea as to the value which could be higher or lower.

Step #2) Identify Similar Interior Features

The home you're comparing to must have similar quality features and interior. If a home has a very modern interior, elevators, high-tech kitchen, and other amenities - this can increase the value of the property exponentially. This is why you shouldn't compare "fixed" properties to a ran down property. A qualified comp should have identical interior features to the property you're considering purchasing. If you buy a semi-ran-down property, find semi-ran-down comps in similar shape. If you buy a well-maintained property, find other well-maintained properties. The closer a property is to your purchase, the higher the accuracy of the value appraisal.

Step #3) Identify Similar Square Footages

The home must be of similar or identical square footage to be considered a comp. If you're buying a 2000 sq ft. home you won't get a lot of insight comparing that to a 5000 sq. ft. home. Try to narrow down comps based on the size of the home and follow that up by removing the difference. Let's say a 2000 sq. ft home goes for $100,000 in an area. If you see 4000 sq ft. homes going for $200,000-250,000 in that same area, you can easily determine the average home value. Square footage is usually the biggest value-indicator.

4) Identify Similar Constructions

Construction type can affect the house price as many construction methods have changed over the years. This is particularly true in states such as Florida where after Hurricane-regulations, many new homes are now Hurricane-proof and command higher real-estate prices than old homes. The structure also reflects in the home insurance prices as outdated homes will command much higher insurance or be refused by the insurers outright. Analyze when the comps were built and the structural difference between your property and the way those differences reflect in the final price.

Real Estate Websites For Comps

Which tools are the best for gathering data? Analyze local properties by looking at the biggest real estate websites that can give you a list of "Sold" properties, home value estimates for each neighborhood and current listings. The following websites are the most reliable tools for the house-flipper:

Zillow

Zillow is currently the largest real-estate website in the United States. Zillow exclusively specializes in the US real-estate market and can give you detailed value estimates for every house in the US. The company operates on a map-based principle and once you've narrowed in on a location, it can estimate the value of each house by the average listing price and sold price in the area + indicators such as square footage taken by government data. The company makes researching properties in your area a breeze, and it can narrow them down by price + give you access to public records and recently sold properties in every area. Zillow is actually getting into house-flipping themselves and their agents are tasked to sell each property in less than 3 months: It's the go-to website for a house-flipper because their database is the largest.

Trulia

Trulia is an excellent tool for house-flippers because it provides insight that might affect the home value such as "local insights". These insights can make you aware of things you didn't realize on-location while you were looking at a property: Crime reports, school ratings, local community events, and the website even has discussion boards. A home-flipper can have a big-picture perspective on their acquisition by using Trulia's detailed analysis of each property.

Redfin

Redfin is a popular real estate tool: It's main standout feature is the 3D walk-through feature that enables you to look at properties "inside the home" by walking around as if you were on location. They have relatively low listing fees too. However, this tool does not have the extensive analysis features of Zillow and Trulia.

Realtor.com

Realtor.com used to be the biggest real estate listing site and it currently holds its own by providing one of the most accurate value appraisal tools that can identify current home value for each home in the US. The site also has tracking tools for real estate investors that can track your profits.

Hiring An Appraiser

Once you've gathered your comps, analyzed properties using online tools, consulted with realtors - the final step you should take is to hire a professional appraiser who can walk in the property and analyze everything for a final estimate. They can give you a non-biased perspective as to the real value of the home. If your comps and research come close to that of the appraiser, you can be certain you're getting a great price!

Pro Tip: Appraisers provide different value-insight than realtors or online tools. They analyze the home by stepping inside and testing all the individual features. They will analyze the property location, structural layout/convenience, required improvements for the bathrooms/kitchen, HVAC conditions which might require repairs, and the condition of the interior/exterior. Once they've had all these things in account and ran their calculations, they will give you a final estimate. The appraiser puts the final piece of the puzzle together as they can summarize their calculation and you can compare that to the data you've gathered online. To find an appraiser, either consult with realtor for a referral or Google local appraisers.

Step On The The Property

There is nothing that can indicate whether your property will sell or not than actually setting foot on the property: You'll instantly know if it "feels right" or if the property feels like a bad deal the second you step on the property yourself! Ask yourself: Would you live on this property? Put yourself in the shoes of a customer and decide if you would live in that property and which upgrades you'd want for yourself. Do you feel safe in the area? Do you like the shape of the house? What bothers you about the interior? If you make the property livable for yourself, there is a high chance someone else will find it livable as well.

Following the 70% Rule

Flipping Houses

You must choose between 2 properties: The first costs $100,000 and has a bad interior and the second costs $115,000 but has a decent interior? Which one should you buy and flip? How do you estimate how much you should pay for a property once you've narrowed down the neighborhood research and know the average going value per square foot? The answer is the 70% rule! The 70% rule is the rule-of-thumb for house-flippers because it leave 30% profit at the end of each flip that you can use to cover your lending fees and other small/unplanned costs. A house-flipper is not "safe" because they're always prone to unexpected charges and the 70% rule ensures your investment is safe from structural failures, delayed repair charges, takeover fees and more. Novices make the mistake of buying a house without accounting for the 70% rule, and then they either make no profit or they even lose money. This is why smart house-flippers calculate all their final profits and expenses before they even purchase a house.

How Does The 70% Rule Work?

To avoid over-bidding or loss of profits, the 70% rule can help you determine the maximum you should spend on each property. If a house is going to be worth $100,000 at the end, you probably shouldn't be bidding even half of that amount at the start. The 70% rule is applied before flippers put down a bid on a property. Flippers must do their calculations 3 months in advance in order to determine the ARV (final sale price) and take away 70% of that which is the maximum they should spend on an unfixed property. There is a simple formula which a flipper can use to run the basic calculations.

Pro Tip: Remember that what you pay at the start is the biggest indicator as to how much profit you'll be left with post-flip. If you overpay for the property, you will make less profits for yourself and your investors. However, if you bid below the 70% max-value and you negotiate a property for less than that amount, you're likely to be left with huge profits at the end of the flip. Therefore, your job is to estimate what 70% ARV is for a particular property, take that away and negotiate the house for that amount and/or less.

What Is The 70% Formula?

The 70% rule is a formula to determine the maximum price you should be paying for a house pre-flip. The 70% rule applies for properties on all levels: abandoned homes, normal homes in working-class areas and even high-value homes in class-A neighborhoods. The 70% in essence dictates that an investor should not pay more than 70% of the final value post-renovations. This leaves investors with a 30% surplus that comprises their final profit and other miscellaneous costs that might arise. The 70% rule functions on the principle of ARVL: After repair value. Once you've added-up the total renovation costs on top of the original home value - you have your ARV. You then subtract 70% from that ARV and you have the maximum figure you should pay for the property. If we apply simple math, and the ARV of a house is $100,000 and it needs $30,000 in repairs, this means that the investor should not pay more than $40,000 for that property. We'll take a detailed look at the math below.

The 70% rule is a general rule, however, it's not written in stone. You can technically flip a house at no-profit to show yourself that flipping houses is possible. You could try to invent your own 60% rule and only bid at 60% of the ARV, which many people will likely take too (if they're in desperate need of liquid).

The Golden 70% Rule Formula

The formula of the 70% rule is the following:

ARV x 70% - Renovation Costs = Max Bid Price

Alternative formula: ARV x 0.70 - Renovation Costs = Max Bid Price

Real estate investing carries hidden costs that are not outright visible such as the initial financing/lender costs, settlement costs, realtor/listing costs, carrying costs and other soft costs such as property taxes, insurance and capital gains taxes. Once you add in unforeseen renovation costs, you must set aside at least 30% in profits to account for all those costs at once. This way you're not caught by surprise when your contractor overbids by $2000 and you can't find a smaller bid but you planned to only spend $500.

Calculations Using The 70% Rule

For the purpose of averages, we'll take the average home value of a United States home: $230,000. How much should you pay for a $230,000 house (if the home is worth $230,000 after renovations)? Let's account for all costs associated with buying a $230K home.

ARV (After-Repair-Value): $230,000.

Renovation Costs: $50,000 (example: $20,000 for a kitchen, $15,000 for a bathroom, and $15,000 for paint, interior upgrades, lawn upgrades, etc).

Renovation Reserve Budget: $10,000 (take away 20% of your total renovation budget as a buffer for unexpected expenses and contractor surcharges - you might not always spend this, but to stay safe!).

Settlement Costs: $10,000.

Finance Costs (Interest Rates): $5000.

Total Costs: $75,000.

The total amount of how much you'll have to set aside to flip the average US home of $230,000 is $75,000 for repair costs. In many cases this can become $65,000 or less if you hire the right contractors, sell the property yourself, spend less on renovations, negotiate better lending rates, etc. The 70% rule is not written in stone, but for the purpose of averages we'll take the estimate of $75,000.

Now let's apply the golden formula:

$230,000 x 0.70 - $75,000 = $86,000

Conclusion: According to the 70% rule, a flipper who wants to flip a home worth $230,000 at the end should not bid more than $86,000 - however, that's not how it works in practice because it doesn't account for your estimated profit. Let's say you wish to make a $40,000 profit at the end of this sale. If you started with a $230,000 ARV estimate and you took away your $75,000 expenses and then you took away your estimated profits of $40,000, you would reach a maximum bid price of $115,000. You could make the $40,000 profit by offering anything less than $115,000, but it's possible to make more if you bid lower and spend less on renovations and miscellaneous costs. The final profit will be based on the extensiveness of your renovations, your experience negotiating and flipping, the risk level and the time the deal takes.

Warning: Do not over-estimate the ARV. The 70% Rule only helps you identify instant costs, but it will never reflect the actual repair costs once you're on the ground because each property requires unique treatment. Always be cautious and conservative with your ARV estimates and use worst-case-scenario numbers for your renovation costs. You won't be able to get inside a property and estimate repairs if you're buying a foreclosed home, and this is something to consider when you're on the hunt for good deals. You'll have to run those calculations in advance.

Is it a Buyer's, Seller's, or Balanced Market?

Flipping Houses

You've seen the millions people make on TV: flippers snatch up properties and flip them fast. How can you tell if the market is a seller's/flipper's market or if it's a buyer's market? There are ways to determine if the market shifts towards buyers or sellers more. For instance, once the US economy crashed in 2008, the market was considered a "buyers" market. Home prices that used to be through-the-roof suddenly reached abysmal prices and wealthy individuals with access to capital could snatch them up for the low.

Once the housing market crashes, the market becomes a buyer's market and it's very hard to flip a property for a profit. However, when the economy strengthens and money is flowing everywhere this becomes a seller's market and it's actually harder for buyers to afford the homes. Housing prices are further solidified by foreign investors trying to get a foothold in the US and investing in property. The median home value in the US is $231,000, however, in states like California it's over $500,000. A strong economy can be a negative for flippers because it's harder to find foreclosed properties at a low price. How do we determine if the market is currently a buyer's, seller's or balanced market?

The 3 Types Of Real Estate Markets

At the end of each fiscal year, statistics agencies can determine if the market was a buyer's, seller's or balanced one. Example: Gross returns on house flips are different every year. In 2018 the average gross return was 44% and it was 50% in 2017. Why the decrease in average gross returns? The economy strengthens and less people go bankrupt. This means that less properties go on the market at foreclosed prices, hence flippers invest less because it becomes harder to find "great deals". This is neither bad or good, as an experienced flipper can find excellent deals under every possible market. The metric only displays the change in the market to help you understand why certain things happen when they happen.

#1) Seller's Market: If the market is a seller's market (a flipper is a seller too!), this means that there is a surplus in demand and a lack in supply. To imagine the best example a seller's market, think of San Francisco, CA. Each apartment that goes on sale in San Francisco is sold in a matter of days and many people enter bidding wars for the chance to purchase a living space. This is because San Francisco is a tech hub with some of the highest average salaries in the US. Despite that, the city refuses to provide building permits for high-rise buildings that would enable developers to build housing for people moving in the city. This means that living space becomes scarce and real estate and rent prices skyrocket. San Francisco is an extreme example of a seller's market, but in general if demand is high then that is a strong indicator of a seller's market.

#2) Buyer's Market: A buyer's market is when the inventory of housing surpasses that of the demand. Have you driven past empty new suburban developments that are not inhabited yet? In many cases this is an indicator of a buyer's market, as the need for housing exceeds the demand. This means that buyer's are in a superior position to sellers because they have plenty to choose from and they can even low-ball sellers for a decreased price. It is very hard to make a profit when you're in a buyer's market. Take a look at the city you're investing in. Are there many vacant new developments? Do new developments sell out fast? If the city is full of vacant properties and has a surplus of developments, it will be harder to sell a property. In the worst case scenario a property can sit on the market for a full year.

#3) Balanced Market: A balanced market means that inventory and demand are equalized and that for each new development there are adequate customers. The United States has been a balanced market for most of its history and the only exceptions were strong economic downshifts/recessions or micro-bubbles within certain regions that experience an economic boom. The economy of a city can have a strong impact on the real estate market and in the most extreme examples such as Detroit and San Francisco, we see either a complete collapse or an over inflation of the housing prices. In a typical balanced market, there is a 6 month advance on inventory that meets demand.

Best Market For House-Flips & Hot Markets

The best-case-scenario for a house-flipper is a seller's market. When there is a high demand for housing in a thriving city, it's a lot easier to flip a property. If no one wants to live in a city and demand for housing is low, it will be a lot harder to flip a property because selling properties is hard in general. In a balanced market, it's possible to make a healthy amount of money flipping houses.

Labor costs are affected by a shortage of workers: If there are less qualified workers to carry out tasks, the contractors will require more money. However, this depends on the local market and some markets are less impacted by labor shortages. Research your local market for contractor prices and compare them to the US average. Some markets have lower labor costs. The expenses that go into renovations will be a major factor in your bottom line.

The fastest growing cities in the US will have the highest demand for housing. The urban areas and immediate suburbs of those cities are ideal for house-flipping because they are almost always seller's markets. Think the fastest growing cities in the US are New York City and/or Los Angeles? Wrong! Per capita, the fastest growing cities are usually mid-sized cities with a strong economy. Cities such as Seattle, Austin, Denver, Omaha, Miami and Raleigh top the list as the fastest growing cities in the nation. These cities can grow as much as 15%

each 5 years. Where will all those people live? It's up to you to provide them a living space. With a strong job market and growing wages, many people can now afford a down-payment on a property. This is why "hot" real estate markets are either seller's markets or balance markets. It's up to you to take advantage and make a healthy profit on your first flip.

Chapter 3 - No Money, No Problem

Wholesaling: All You Need to Know to Get Started

Novices think they need a $120,000/yr income and a real estate license to get funding for their flips – they're wrong! We're about to distill multiple ways to acquire capital without doing it the conventional way. The spirit of house-flipping kicks in at this stage: The excitement of a research, acquisition and gathering liquid to finance your first deal. Are you ready to make your first acquisitions and research houses to buy? Are you ready to become a property owner and get the keys to your first flip? Hold on, because we're about to break down the most unconventional and secret ways to obtain funding.

The first of such methods is "wholesaling". The name "wholesale" rings bells if you ever step into the mall at Christmas - all the stores are selling merchandise at low prices to get rid of off-season stock. In real estate, wholesaling refers to virtually the same thing - getting deals off the main market. The main real estate market is the market we all see: the classified ads online, the real estate websites. Wholesaling strives to buy real estate off the main market - you can purchase your first house from wholesalers.

How To Flip A House With No Money?

It sounds like an advertising leading you on - it's not! Wholesaling can enable you to purchase properties off-market for a much lower value than they would sell on the main market. Wholesaling is low-risk because you directly contact the owner of the property to purchase their property at a discount - and once you flip it, you share the profits. This means that you never take title, i.e. you never officially become the "owner" of the property but you reap the profits at the end. You don't bear responsibility for the property and you make a spread once the property sells for a fee you agree with in advance.

Positives/Negatives Of Wholesaling

Wholesaling is the fastest method to finance and flip a property without having a lot of capital available. However, it does require more expertise and networking than a conventional house-flip.

Positives Of Wholesaling:

✓Flip houses without little/no capital.

✓No down payments or less legal fees as you never take ownership of the property.

✓Safer than conventional forms of real estate investing.

✓Ability to finance multiple deals at once.

✓Credit score is irrelevant.

Disadvantages Of Wholesaling:

✗Requires social acuity, networking and knowledge about the whole process.

✗Must seek out investors who will bankroll the deals.

✗Must plan out an exit strategy for a property you don't own.

✗If you don't finance the deal you will make less than the investor.

How Wholesaling Works

Wholesaling is house-flipping WITHOUT taking ownership of the property. Wholesalers discover a house seller who agrees to partner with them and allow them to acquire the house at a low price. This effectively makes the wholesaler act as the "middle man" between the owner and the future buyer. This is ideal for beginners because it decreases the risk of things going wrong and them being stuck with a house. Wholesaling is ideal for beginners, however, new wholesalers should consult real estate attorneys for all assignment contingencies. It's on you to select how much you'll charge in "assignment fees" which are your profits for acting as the middleman financier.

How To Determine If Wholesaling Is For You

If you have the know-how to seek-out investors who can put up the initial money for renovations and you know how to find property owners who would agree to a flip deal, you are ideal for wholesaling. This method is perfect for people who like to network and can put people together on a deal. Start on Linkedin to build local connections to people involved in house-flipping finance and real-estate. Your job as a wholesaler is to learn your local market, develop connections, know about the cost of repairs and cut a deal with the investors.

Essentially, you don't need any money to start wholesaling! You can network with financiers who will put up the money for the house-purchase and the renovations, find a person willing to sell their house at a discount without taking title, and flip the house. You will have to carry out the same repairs as if you financed and repaired the house yourself, but you will be taking other people's money and directing it for the highest investment-profit ROI.

Calculating Profit For Wholesaling

To operate as wholesaler, you must develop a wholesale mindset - you can't apply the same principles as a regular flipper because many properties won't work as wholesales. As a rule of thumb, you should seek to identify properties that can work as wholesales and the following formula applies:

ARV * 70% - repair cost - your fee = Offer you give.

Flipping Houses

Take out your calculator now! Let's make an example at an average $125,000 house that requires $25,000 in repairs for a total re-sell value of $150,000. What would your final profit be and how much should you offer the house owner to make that profit?

$150,000 (after-repair value) * 70% - $25,000 (repair cost) - $15,000 (your wholesaling fee) = $65,000.

Your maximum offer for this house should be $65,000. If you want to close it instantly you should consider lowering your wholesaling fee to $10,000 to offer the property-owner $70,000 for the house. In both cases, you're free to decide the wholesaling fee based on how much you think the owner would agree to. If the property owners are open to negotiation, you should set a higher fee. If they act stingy and refuse to sell, offer them a lower wholesaling fee. The final offer will determine how much you can take home: if you offer less, you will take more profit. If you offer more, you will take less profit. Determine if the profit on a wholesale is worth all the effort you'll put in the property.

Warning: Research the property owner to determine if the property owners owe too much before you offer them a deal, because in many cases they won't give you a good deal if they're in severe debt. Good deals are possible if both parties see a profit, not at the expense of the other party.

Once you've identified a deal you have to sign a separate "wholesaling contract" which will entitle you to fix up the property and ultimately sell it for a profit - once it's sold the previous owner has to move out. Real estate lawyers who specialize in this law practice can ensure the escrow funds and transactions are carried out in an efficient manner. Wholesale contracts are taken up by real estate professionals who flip properties for a living - professionals like you. It's your job to identify eligible properties, negotiate a deal with the seller, renovate the property and sell it for a profit.

How to Get a Hard Money Loan

Think you need to spend months guaranteeing the bank you will pay back your loans? Are you struggling to gather all the evidence your bank loan manager asks before he approves your loan? What about time - do you have all the paperwork but the bank still takes months to approve your loans? Hard money loans help you get around that. Your loan can be approved in as little as 7 days and the average approval time is less than 10 days. This allows the lender to analyze the property and determine if it will make a profit before approving your loan. "Fix and flip" lending is how thousands of properties are sold each month, and this lending enables flippers who are always on the lookout for the next deal to finance their next property. Don't wait to finish your current project before you gather more finances - you can apply for multiple loans at once and fix up multiple properties. While you're working on your current property, you could line up the next one.

Hard money loans are real-estate loans for flippers who require fast access to capital without consulting banks. Banks have rigid approval procedures that take weeks or even months - hard money loans are issued within days, effectively allowing flippers to capitalize on current investments while bankrolling multiple properties at once. Hard money loans are for flippers who want to invest in multiple properties and require fast approval procedures. If you want to flip multiple properties at once without wasting months before financing new properties, this loan type is for you.

Sound too good to be true? Hard money loans do have higher interest rates but they cater to a certain demographic of flippers who can afford to pay higher interest rates because the speed makes up for the surcharge on interest. Time is of the essence here: The faster you flip your property, the less you pay in interest. If you can flip properties fast you will reap higher rewards. Hard money loans, also known as "fix and flip" loans allow you to get in and out of the market fast and secure the capital you need to renovate and sell a property.

Pro Tip: Prepare your property acquisition documents in advance as "fix and flip" loans require detailed documentation to expedite approval. This part takes the most and once your loan is approved (usually within days) you can purchase the property and start working.

Advantages Of Hard Money Loans:

✓Only 10% down-payment required: Can finance 90% of the property acquisition cost and 100% of all renovations.

✓No upfront contracts or costs pre-approval.

✓Average approval time of 7-10 days (45 days for conventional bank loans).

✓All types of real estate accepted (houses, condos, commercial properties, etc).

✓Can apply with bad credit history, past bankruptcies or back taxes owed.

Disadvantages of hard-money loans:

✗4-5% higher interest than conventional loans. The average interest rate is 5-8%.

Hard Money Loans VS Conventional Bank Loans

The main advantage of hard money loans is that they approve loans based on the asset in question - not the borrower. The conventional bank will analyze your personal employment, finances, job history, credit score and account for your personal liability. Hard money lenders only care for the property: They want to know the property will flip and sell. The entire focus is on the property. Hard money loans are catered to flippers and provide coverage for all flipper's needs: purchase costs, closing costs, legal costs, permit costs, and renovations. In hard money loans, the all-around financing is called "asset based underwriting" - this is the main advantage over conventional loans. Hard money loans are available to people with bad or limited credit histories, as the focus is put on the deals themselves, not the person.

Wouldn't it be great if all banks only looked at your deals and decided to finance projects based on which one seems most profitable instead of digging in your personal history? This is the essence of hard money loans - while banks would consider it risky to invest in the house-flipping business, fix-and-flip loans thrive on volatile investments such as flipping because they bankroll the entire project and know that the property is guaranteed to make a profit (based on market research and other metrics conducive to the ARV of the property). They also don't exclude people with a history of bad credit. Even if your current credit score is good, a bank will outright refuse you if you had a bankruptcy under your belt. Asset-lending is secured by the collateral and the lenders are not in danger as they can acquire the property if you fail to flip it and make payments. However, they are also open to finance all your endeavors and help you gather the finances you need to make the property shine.

Pro Tip: Time is your main ally in hard money loans. If a property looks too shabby and your intuition tells you it's going to take months to fix it - ditch it. You need a solid property that you can flip within a few weeks by upgrading basics such as the bedrooms, bathrooms, kitchens and/or paint. The faster you get rid of the property, the less you pay in interest. This is further expedited if you have your documents in place, as your loan can be approved in as little as a week.

How To Get A Hard Money Loan?

Start by gathering all your paperwork related to the property. This includes your current finances, the property value, research, calculations in terms of repairs and your profit expectations. The lenders will ask you for documentation and might inquire as to your personal history as an investor. Answer questions honestly! If you've never flipped a property, tell them this is your first flip. Preparing the documentation and gaining approval takes the most time - make sure you're prepared in advance.

What Are The Interest Rates?

The interest rates on hard money loans are on average 4% higher than on regular bank loans - this is actually a great deal considering the speed and low personal standards they impose for applying for a loan. In essence, you're paying a 4-5% premium on the interest for faster access to capital which enables you to finance multiple properties at once. The applications also require a lot less underwriting. The focus is put on the property itself: If you can prove the property will be profitable for the lenders, they will secure you a loan.

Is the process that much faster? Why pay 4% more in interest when you can wait for a bank loan? The answer is simple: If you want speed, you pay a premium for the privilege. Banks are reliable institutions for financing properties, but banks will analyze your credit history and the average approval for a bank loan is 45 days (close to 2 months). If you can wait 2 months for a loan to be approved, you should opt for the lower interest rates of a bank. In essence, banks are better for people who have excellent credit ratings and plan to flip very few properties each year. Hard money loans are for people who want to flip a dozen properties every year and don't want to wait months for approval on each loan.

The biggest advantage of "fix-and-flip" loans is that lenders understand flippers. Lenders know that the essence of house-flipping is about the asset itself and they invest based on the deal - not about who you are and how your past divorce caused you to go bankrupt. If you present a great deal such as a fixable property that requires little renovations but has potential of selling, you are almost guaranteed to receive a hard money loan. If you have previous experience flipping properties, your loans could be approved in less than a week.

Flipping Houses With No Money Using Private Investors

Are you scared to approach financiers who would bankroll your property? Worry not - we'll teach you how to locate private lenders to finance your property. Private lending is in essence reaching out to people who have money to finance your flip when you don't have money. A private lender could technically be your relative or your father in law. However, in most cases private lenders are established businessmen who invest their assets in local, high-risk investments. Private lenders are individual partners who bankroll the flip of a property - this type of lending is similar to "fix-and-flip" loans but you deal with individuals in person instead of financial institutions.

Private lending is a form of obtaining capital from individuals who specialize in lending to flippers. Lenders who bankroll properties tend to be wealthy and established individuals that you can reach out to and obtain funding in person. What's in it for them? They get a cut at the end of each flip, and their cut is usually bigger than that of bank loans. Private lenders don't care about your credit score but they want you to have a track record of flipping properties before they write you a 6-figure check for your newest flip. To secure their investment, lenders make flippers sign a "first deed of trust" agreement (mortgage) which means their money is secured by a hard asset (the property purchased).

Who Is Qualified For A Private Loan?

Each individual who want to flip properties can reach out to investors for a private loan. There are no minimum finances or minimum credit scores required. However, to get an investor the main "qualifier" for you would be your past experience and track record. Dealing with private lenders is only recommended for people who have flipped at least one property, because many of them won't engage with novices.

Flipping Houses

They want to know their investment is secure before they put down a six-figure payment for your new property. Your chances of being successful with private lenders will be exponentially higher if you have a history of flipping properties in the past.

Pro Tip: Start with a regular bank loan and flip your first property using low-risk bank loans. Once you've flipped your first property, most fix-and-flip lenders and private-money lenders will approve your loans. You will then be able to flip multiple properties at the same time (as you already have a 'track record' of flipping properties).

What Are Private Lenders?

Private lenders aren't always retired wealthy individuals who you meet at the Country Club – you can now find private lenders on LinkedIn. Private lenders can also be "investment groups" or "partnership groups" that finance real estate deals; this will depend on your city/state and financial options available. In most cases private lenders provide direct finances: Whatever amount you estimate you'll need for the acquisition and repair costs, they'll bankroll it. However, they also collect their cut which you'll have to negotiate at the start. The main advantage with private lenders is that many times they won't even ask you for a down payment, but they only trust flippers with a past track record.

How To Get A Private Loan?

This is where the fun part kicks in - you don't even need a down payment with private lenders. It's possible to combine two funding sources: One that will finance the purchase/repair price (but ask for a down payment) and another lender who will finance the down payment for the original loan. It's possible to obtain funding from two lenders who will finance your deal, and at the end of the sale distribute the profits equally and accordingly to each investor. What you have is "sweat equity": You identify an attractive real-estate deal and you carry out the rehab and selling process on your own. The lenders use their resource to finance your purchase.

Private lending can work in multiple ways, however, the two most common are the following:

1) Two partners join together: One handles the financing (supplies the funding) and the other discovers a deal, carries out repairs and sells the property.

2) Three partners join together: One handles the financing, the other handles the down payment for the financing and the third (you) handles the property.

How To Find Qualified Private Investors

To make private deals run smoothly, you will have to identify whether the person you're doing business with is qualified to provide the financing for your flip. The following 3 traits are what separate good investors from bad investors:

1. Access to wealth/resources. A private lender has to be a wealthy individual who invests in many flippers like yourself, and this shouldn't be their first investment. The profile of private lenders is usually established, middle aged or older business owners.

2. Transparent communications. Private lenders will be eager to discuss the details of the acquisition and all the construction/repair costs, including the final sale price. They will be transparent about the purchase and tell you exactly how much they can finance and what their cut is at the end.

3. Separation of roles. The investor has to realize your sweat equity and the amount of effort/work you put into the property - this way there is no confusion as to the scope of work involved or how much you deserve at the end of the sale.

There are many ways to source out private lenders, but the best way to start is to find lenders located in your area.

Researching Lenders In Your Area

The best way to start is by networking: Attend real-estate events and seminars and meet people in "the business". They will be able to put you in touch with investors and you should be able to meet them in person at these events. However, if you don't have time to network or don't know how to you can also look up local county records for all properties that will include the closed rate, the interest and the lender's contact details. Look up who lent out in your vicinity within the last 3-6 months as those lenders are likely active on the market.

Once you've accumulated a list of investors/lenders, you should directly reach out to them. Most lenders leave their email, but you can make a stronger impression by cold-calling them and pitching them a deal.

Example: "Hello, is this lender [name]? My name is [your name] and I see that you've lent out money for this project on 94 Street, Nashville. My company does fix-up projects and I'm calling to see if you're interested in one more of these deals".

There are no rules as to how the conversation is supposed to flow – this is about your personal relationship with the lender. The wisest option is to talk about how you flipped houses in the past to get the investor comfortable with how you do business. Do everything you can to establish rapport and make them comfortable by discussing their projects, the scope of deals they do, their town, family or even sports. The more comfortable they feel with you as a person, the more willing they'll be to finance your projects.

Chapter 4 - Choosing the Right Property

Key Factors For Choosing The Right Location

Location, location, location! People would rather invest $250,000 in a house in a good neighborhood than spend $150,000 on a house in a bad neighborhood (even if they can afford both!). Have you ever driven to a friend's place and thought "Wow, this is a good area?". If the roads are in good shape, houses look maintained and there are nearby amenities you assume that it's a good, safe neighborhood. How do you feel when you drive past a neighborhood with bad houses, shanty roads full of potholes, unlit street lights and bulletproof-sealed convenience stores? You instantly want to get out! House-flipping is not about choosing the first $30,000 "deal" that comes your way. Certain neighborhoods always have low property values for a reason and they're much more prone to crime. Once you arrive at the location of your flip and you get a personal taste of the neighborhood, you can immediately identify the class of neighborhood it is. This is why you must always investigate properties by visiting them instead of relying on online research.

Classes Of Neighborhoods

There are 4 classes of neighborhoods in real estate: A-class, B-class, C-class and D-class. Similar to a school grading system, in real estate neighborhoods are rated based on property value, location and overall condition. Think of it this way: The most desirable neighborhoods are the class A neighborhoods. The least desirable ones are the class D neighborhoods, and class D includes abandoned properties.

Class A neighborhoods are the kind of houses every family wishes to live in: They're the epitome of the American Dream. Class B and C neighborhoods are more or less "average" neighborhood: Class B/C are slightly outdated, many of them are in bad shape but they're generally safe and habitable. Class D neighborhoods are crime-ridden, the houses are in bad shape, and they command low property values. We avoid class D neighborhoods for the purpose of house-flipping because even a renovated property in those neighborhoods can sit on the market for long. For the purpose of maximizing profits, we focus on class B and class C neighborhoods where we can snatch up properties on the low and renovate them.

Pro Tip: There is no government organization that "officially" classifies neighborhoods. You must differentiate classes based on your own knowledge and intuition.

1) Class A Neighborhoods

Class A neighborhoods are new affluent and safe neighborhoods. Those include the "elite" mansions and high-HOA communities, but they also include very new developments. Have you driven past a spanking new, shiny suburb that has all-new properties, access to good schools, security patrols, restaurants, and other first-class amenities? That is your typical class A neighborhood. Many of them are new and built in the last 10 years, which is why the maintenance is very low and the property value per square foot is the highest. Typically interiors consist of high-tech amenities such as granite countertops, "smart" curtains, hardwood floors, expensive finishes and pools. Class A neighborhoods make good rental investments, but they are not the best for flipping because many of them are already "renovated" and the flipper will have to fork out serious cash to upgrade those houses.

2) Class B Neighborhoods

Class B is actually similar to class A – Class B houses have the same amenities and high-quality infrastructure, but they tend to be older. Class B neighborhoods are safe with access to good schools, hospitals and shopping options. Class B neighborhoods are typically populated by middle-income citizens and they have very few citizens who struggle and live paycheck to paycheck. The typical house in a class B neighborhood is 30 years old and in good shape. If any repairs are required they will typically be lower than those of Class C and D neighborhoods. In essence, a class B neighborhood is a slightly older and downgraded version of a class A neighborhood.

3) Class C Neighborhoods

Class C neighborhoods are lower-income neighborhoods where the infrastructure tends to be outdated, the houses are old and in bad shape and the residents are typically low-income. Many residents of class C neighborhoods will be on government subsidies and struggling to get by. Class C neighborhoods are not as unsafe as class D neighborhoods, but their safety is a lot worse compared to prime Class A and B neighborhoods. Typical signs of a class C neighborhood include bad maintenance of lawns, extra security around houses, pawn shops/liquor stores, cash checking businesses, weapons stores, etc. Most houses in class C neighborhoods are at least 30+ years old and can be over 50 years old. They will require heavy repairs, but the price difference between these homes and Class B homes can be significant and worth a flip.

4) Class D Neighborhoods

Class D neighborhoods don't exist in every city but they are easy to recognize: Abandoned buildings, decaying old infrastructure, unlit streets, gang presence, visible drug sales and constant police presence. In many cases police is afraid to enter class D neighborhoods themselves. Even public infrastructure such as schools can be abandoned with squatters inside and all working convenience stores have bulletproof windows and armed employees who work behind 3 foot glass. In many cases, class D neighborhoods should be avoided even if they're extraordinarily cheap. Once the renovations are carried out, it will be harder to sell or even rent out the property because it's in a dangerous area. Unless you specialize in flipping class D properties and don't feel threatened by the areas, you should generally avoid flipping properties in such locations.

Flipping Houses

Factors That Increases Property Value

The following things need to be checked on your list to ensure the property you flip will command a high resell value:

✓**Parks/green spaces**. If the property is located near a park or a green space such as woods/hiking trails this can increase property value up to 20%.

✓**School districts**. If the property is located in a good public school district, this can increase property values by 20%. Surveyed buyers say they would pay up to 20% for a home in a good school district.

✓**Medical facilities**. If the property is located close to hospitals this will increase the property value.

✓**Maintenance levels**. The maintenance level of the neighborhood such as road condition, sidewalks, street lights, cleanliness, maintained yards, etc, can increase the property value significantly. In HOA communities this is handled by a single institution and residents only pay monthly fees.

✓**Recreation/shopping**. If the property is located near restaurants, shopping malls, recreation centers and other entertainment options this will increase property value.

✓**Walkability**. If the home is located in a walkable area where clients can walk to convenience stores, this increases property value. If a car is required for a trip to the store, this can negatively impact the property value.

✓**Public transportation (only for urban areas).** In urban areas access to public transportation such as bus stops and metro stations can increase property value.

Factors That Decrease Property Value

What are "hidden" value killers that sellers don't advertise on realtor ads? What if you see an epic deal and you're ready to put down a payment, only to learn there's a reason why it's that cheap? The following things can decrease property value significantly:

✘**Airports**. If the property is located next to an airport it will have constant noise from airplanes taking off and landing. Airplanes are noise machines and flights usually land 24/7 which makes rest impossible.

✘**Train station/metro station**. Trains produce a squeaky noise and if a property is located near a train station or a metro, the owners will be able to hear trains passing by the whole day.

✘**Fire department/PD**. If the property is located near a fire department or a police station, they will witness activity and patrol cars making noise around the clock - this decreases the value of a property.

✘**Highways nearby**. If the property is located next to a major highway the passing cars will produce noise 24/7 which decreases the quality of life for residents. Many local governments put up noise barriers on highways but that usually doesn't block out all the noise.

✘**Nightlife establishments**. If the property is located near nightlife establishments such as clubs/bars this can affect the quality of life for residents and lower property value.

Noise pollution is the #1 property-price killer because it decreases the quality of life for people residing in houses near noisy establishments.

Take Action - Visit The Property!

When you research your neighborhood, online data is does not cut it – you must visit the property yourself. Don't just drive to the property in a rush! Take a spin across the street and analyze the nearby streets. Does the neighborhood feel safe, are there people walking around, are children playing freely, are the street lights working, are the lawns trimmed, are the houses in good shape, are there local schools and amenities? These are all things you will discover in less than one hour of observing a neighborhood. It will give the last bit of reassurance you need before you put down a house payment.

Features to Look For & Features to Avoid in Property

What is the difference between buying a cheap property and renovating it vs. buying a normal-priced property and renovating it? Are you falling to the temptation of buying the first $30,000 house you see in your city? The price cannot make up for things you can't fix – it's important to analyze the features first. Here's how most novices mess up:

Expectation: You will buy a $30,000 house and spend $50,000 renovating it and you'll conclude your first flip. You're now a profitable house-flipper!

Reality: The repairs now take too long, you can't do anything without a permit, you wait for inspector meetings, your repairs are delayed and it takes forever. You lose money!

How do you identify properties that take little cosmetic fixes which you can renovate in a month, without waiting for inspections, permits and dealing with other legal hurdles? These are things you have to look out for before you purchase a property. In general, you want to avoid projects that seem too "difficult" to add or change anything. You want to focus on simple cosmetic upgrades. If the property is too far run down, it will be impossible to fix unless you spend months on it. If the property is in good shape, you can get away with as little as a few cosmetic upgrades such as the paint-job. If the property is in decent shape and has good features, you'll find it easy to fix and sell on the market. If the property is hard to fix, it will be impossible to fix, lose you time on permits and sit on the market longer.

Pro Tip: The golden rule of identifying properties is to find "easy to fix" properties. If a property looks easy to fix, you should snatch it instantly. If the property is too far gone, seek out better properties.

Factors That Sell A Property

The following are the most sought-after features in a property. Prior to putting down a payment on a house, you should find one that ticks all boxes or come close to the ideal:

✓**Large bedrooms**. The best-selling houses are houses with 3 bedrooms. That is a typical American house. Seek out a house with a large master bedroom that can house a king sized bed and has space to walk around it. The secondary bedrooms should be large enough to accommodate a queen sized bed or two small beds. The first thing people look for is the number of bedrooms - the more bedrooms you have the better. Find houses that have spacious master bedrooms.

✓**Multiple bathrooms**. As a rule-of-thumb the house should have at least 1 bathroom for each floor. If you have a house with 2 floors and there's only one bedroom, move on. The same holds true for half-bathrooms, each floor has to have a full bathroom. This is valuable for families that have multiple members. If a house has more bathrooms, the owner will be able to host parties and when their house is "full" they will need multiple bathrooms. Do you wonder why big mansions have 10-15 bathrooms? They need the space for parties where 200-300 people gather in the mansion at once.

✓**Navigable layout**. If you enter the house and you have a bathroom in front of you, you will not have a good impression of a home. The home has to feel "open" and easy to navigate without tight spaces. A bad layout can be fixed if you hire contractors to tear down the walls, but the ideal property is one that doesn't need any walls torn down. Popular layouts include "open kitchen" layouts that have a mini-bar attached to the living room. This makes for easy entertaining.

✓**Garage space**. It goes without saying that a house must have at least a 1-car garage to park the car - people don't like parking in front of their house unless they have to. The ideal garage is a two-car garage. Unless you're going for a luxury property, there is no need to upgrade the garage for more than 2 spaces.

Factors That Delay A Property Sale

Many things can go wrong with your property: You have to do extensive renovations that can be both time-consuming and expensive. This will hurt your budget and extend the time you need until a complete renovation ensues. The local council might require permits for some renovations you have to make - this will mean inspectors arriving at your property, reviewing your renovations, issuing permits that might take forever and then delays in repairs. This will hurt your bottom line and cost you a fortune. How to avoid that? Look for the following signs that hinder renovations and house sales:

✗**Structural issues**. Is the roof of the house unstable and will require a replacement? Are there holes in the foundation of the house? Are the floors uneven? Are there cracks all over the place? All these will require a lot of time and experienced contractors to fix. If the house has structural issues - ditch it.

✗**Outdated designs**. Many houses that were built for older generations are undesirable for today's ones. **Example**: Low ceilings are undesirable and high ceilings over 9 feet are now desirable. Narrow kitchens are a big no no! The modern American wants a wide kitchen where they can move freely and cook their dinner. Any closed-off spaces, low bearing walls and ceilings will be hard to sell.

✗**Uneven bed/bath ratios**. If the house has 4 bedrooms but only 1 bathroom, this means the house was not designed carefully. Seek out houses that have at least 1 bathroom for each 2 bedrooms. If you buy a 4 bedroom house, it should have at least 2 bathrooms or 1.5

bathrooms if you compromise. The bedroom-bathroom ratio should be even and not skewed in favor of bedrooms.

✗ **Inaccessible rooms**. Houses with bad designs will be "closed off" i.e. you won't be able to enter one room without entering another. The ideal house has "open" rooms that can be accessed from main lobbies. **Example**: The master bathroom is only accessible through the master bedroom. This means everyone who wants to go to the bathroom will have to enter the bedroom first. This is a bad design.

'Easy' Repairs That Increase Property Value

Want to make upgrades you can't go wrong with? There are upgrades for all levels - a new bathroom could cost $10,000. A change in the light system can only cost $1000. All repairs depend on what you're trying to fix. In general, you want to focus on cosmetic repairs to increase the value of the property. If your focus is on structural repairs, you will over-spend and your whole budget will be allocated to fixing problems that don't exist on normal properties. The following repairs can reap massive financial rewards:

✓**Paint-jobs**. The go-to fix for every property is a new paint-job. Some paint-jobs will be easy but others might get costly depending on the state of the walls. Start by painting the walls in neutral colors such as white or grey. The paint will cover up any blemishes or patching holes in the walls. This is the easiest upgrade for every property that can boost property value. The exterior paint will depend on what is suitable for the property and neighborhood: Neutral colors are a go-to for exteriors.

✓**New floors and carpets**. Each floor in the house can be replaced with a new, modern hardwood floor. This can be a costly upgrade but it can make a significant difference in the impression people have of a property. New carpets can also add a "premium" feeling to the property, and many of them are affordable. Carpets should be in a neutral color as very light carpets (example: white carpets) will attract dirt and make it visible.

✓**Light fixtures and ceiling fans**. Ceiling fans are very desirable and increase the value of a property - almost 90% of people want a ceiling fan in their home. Light fixtures can be upgraded to modern LED fixtures that operate on "smart" control and can set the vibe of the environment for relaxation. Simple light upgrades can make the home feel modern and sleek.

✓**Interior upgrades**. The interior can change the perception a person has of a house. Interior upgrades such as modern furniture can bring an outdated home to the 21st century. Popular interiors include minimalistic couches, glass/wooden tables, plasma screens and many interiors come in a "package" which helps you revamp the property at once by picking the most suitable one.

✓**Updating infrastructure**. The infrastructure of the house such as the plumbing fixtures which are visible can be updated to newer ones at a low cost. New plumbing fixtures have modern finishes that look great and add a "neat home" feeling.

✓**Landscaping upgrades**. The exterior of the house can improve the "curb appeal" (the first impression people get as they drive by the house). This includes repairing a patchy lawn/making it greener, adding planters, power-washing the whole home, upgrading the entry door, etc. Landscaping will improve the appeal of a house for pictures, making it more upscale and premium looking.

✓**Kitchen/bathroom upgrades**. These are the most expensive upgrades as those two require special treatment compared to living rooms and bedrooms. Most customers expect stainless steel kitchen appliances: fridges, stoves, microwaves, blenders, etc. Simple upgrades such as "smart fridges" can cost thousands of dollars. The upgrades you choose should be set based on your budget.

✓**Window upgrades**. If the windows are outdated, replacing them with new windows can improve the aesthetics of the home. New windows can also increase the energy efficiency of the house, preserving heat in the winter and keeping the home cool in the summer.

Golden Rules for Picking Property

You have $150,000 to invest and your city has hundreds of houses to buy. Even after you narrow your search down to sub $75,000< properties you can still pick out many. How do you choose which one is the right one? How do you know which house will "flip" out of hundreds of houses? The key to selection is to make your calculations in advance! You have to take in account many things: neighborhood, structural integrity, asking price, renovation costs, etc, and you must do it all at once! Many novice flippers barely make a profit or even lose money on their first flip, because they ignore the pre-calculations necessary to be successful in house-flipping. Why would you spend weeks or months toiling with a property only to be left with a miniscule property? It's possible to estimate the profit margins well in advance of purchasing a property (unless you're buying a foreclosed home which you can't see).

Golden Rule #1: The Location Is 50% Of The Flip

In each home flip, the location is 50% of the value and the house is 50% of the value. Location matters as much as the actual house. A property can be in the worst condition: Ran down, outdated, uninhabitable. However, if the property is located in a desirable area (proximity to schools, restaurants, shopping venues and/or scenery) someone will snatch it based on that fact. The location is the most vital bit of research you have to do. Fortunately in this day and age we can analyze houses on Google Street View without ever setting foot on the actual property. Mapping technology and online tools allow us to narrow down a list of properties before visiting in person.

Flipping Houses

There are two things that determine a good location: Scenery and infrastructure. If the house is located near a large body of water, this can dramatically increase the price of the property. Example: An ocean-view house in Malibu might sell for $8M and a highway-view house in the same neighborhood might sell for $4M. This is half price, only because one provides a direct view of the ocean. The closer the house is to oceans, lakes and rivers - the higher the property value. People prefer well-lit houses with views and access to natural light.

If the house has views of mountains, cities or water - it will command higher property rates. However, most houses are located in good-old suburbs. In this case, the only thing that determines home value is infrastructure: State of roads, build quality of houses, maintenance levels, school districts, medical facilities, proximity to amenities and safety. The better a neighborhood, the more expensive the average house is going to be. All properties can be flipped! Million-dollar homes in the hills and ran-down shacks in the ghetto can be flipped on the same principles. The home you need is something in between!

Golden Rule #2) Choose The Worst House In The Best Neighborhood

Based on what you can afford, always opt for the highest-tier neighborhood with the newest houses. Why focus on the better neighborhoods in your budget? They will likely have newer designs that are easy to upgrade and even the worst house in a good neighborhood will be better than an average house in a bad neighborhood. Good neighborhoods will have access to good schools, medical facilities, restaurants, shopping malls, police/PD, highway networks and other first-class amenities that make for a good life.

Pro Tip: No matter how much money you invest in renovations, it will never change the location of the home. Buyers don't want to live in a high-crime area. Pick out the best neighborhood you can find and buy a house in that neighborhood based on your budget.

Golden Rule #3) Buy Cookie Cutter Homes

Always opt for the most average/neutral looking cookie-cutter homes you can find. Why buy that "unique" property? That will exclude a large part of the potential customer pool. If anything feels "odd" about a property (such as the roof has a guitar imprint because the owner was a guitarist) and the property was customized to the demands of a previous owner, avoid it. The property has to look similar to properties in the immediate area. Once clients visit the property they will also look at the properties across the street. If they notice yours stands out, they won't buy it. Even though it sounds harsh in practice, cookie-cutter homes sell fast. Seek out the most average home you can get with nothing unique about it and flip that.

The same applies for your next door neighbors! Make sure there aren't eye-sores in your immediate area. If potential buyers like the home but the home across the street is in bad shape, they will be put off. Does your neighbor dump garbage in front of their house? Do they have their cars parked all over the lawn? Is there a giant boat sticking out their garage? The state of your neighbor's property can affect the value of yours. In essence, you need to find a "normal" home in a "normal" neighborhood. This ensures the home will appeal to the highest number of customers and won't stay on the market for too long.

Golden Rule #4: Avoid Outdated Constructions

Remember the year 1978 - this is the cutoff year for every property you want to purchase. All homes before 1978 used lead based paint and the US "Environmental Protection Agency" changed the paint regulations in that year and which means they consider the possibility that all homes built before 1978 still have lead based paint. In practice, the local government will harass you for documentation on every renovation once they schedule audits. You carefully select pre-approved paints that this will increase your construction costs and make the approval procedure time-consuming. There are certain "guidelines" for all houses built before 1978 that make simple cosmetic fixes like paint-jobs impossible. In addition, the government can fine owners up to $30,000 for not adhering to those regulations.

The layouts of old homes are also a deal-breaker for most new buyers. **Example**: Many old homes have rooms that lead to other rooms and certain rooms are inaccessible from the main lobby. New buyers prefer homes that have "open" floor plans in which each room is accessible independent of other rooms and open-kitchens are also popular. In the past kitchen areas were closed-off with tight space. Current kitchen areas are open and/or adjacent to the living room for easy entertainment.

Golden Rule #5: Flip The House In 3 Months Or Less

The more time spent on renovations, the more it will hurt your wallet. Invest in houses that would take a maximum of 3 months to flip: 1 month for the paperwork and acquisition, 1 month for the renovations and 1 month for the flip. Once you've narrowed down your neighborhoods, the selection should depend on which house would take the least time to fix. If the house seems like it would take more than 1-2 months to renovate, forget about it! If you can renovate a house in less than a month using simple cosmetic fixes (paint, interior decor, landscaping, etc) go for it. If the house has structural problems, each problem could take a month on its own. As a flipper you want to get in and out of deals as fast as possible, leaving you with a sizable profit on each flip.

The longer your house stays on the market the more money you'll have to spend for HOA, insurance, utilities, property taxes, landscaping and/or takeover fees. Houses less than 2000 sq feet are the easiest to renovate because you only renovate 2-3 bedrooms at a time. If the house is large the repairs will take longer and they are more extensive, even if you're only making minor cosmetic repairs.

How to Calculate Your Net Profit

The average gross profit for a house flip in the US is $60,000 - this is before Uncle Sam takes home your income taxes and capital gains taxes apply on assets you've held for less than one year. To calculate the net profit on each flip, you must account for all costs of acquisition: The property purchase, renovation, carrying costs (property taxes, insurance, HOA, utilities, landscape maintenance, closing costs/realtor costs) and then make a deposit on a property. Then, you have to calculate your own individual income taxes based on your state and income levels which you must calculate on your own. For the purpose of this demonstration, we will take an average house flip and calculate all the important costs while explaining what each cost signifies.

Budgeting is essential to successfully flipping the house. The "net" profit in house-flipping refers to the final profit you make after the property is sold - not the income taxes that follow. For example, if your profit at the end of the sale is $40,000 this is considered your "net profit". It is the money that you're left with after you subtract all your renovation expenses, carrying costs and realtor fees.

The Spreadsheet Of Costs

- **Property cost**. This is the largest cost - in many cases the property acquisition price will be 60-70% of your total budget, depending on the renovations you want to carry out. You can lower your purchase price by seeking out deals and foreclosures in your immediate area. Once banks foreclose a property they want to "get rid of it" fast and they sell at under market-value. The less you spend on the property, the more money you'll be left with at the end.
- **Renovation costs**. This will include all the renovations you want to make: paint jobs, interior upgrades, tearing down walls, exterior/landscaping upgrades and more. The renovation costs include the materials required, labor costs and all other surcharges that might arise.

- **Maintenance costs.** Maintenance cost are sometimes referred to as "carrying" costs because one has to pay monthly maintenance on the property including mortgage, utilities, insurance, HOA, and property taxes. The longer your property stays on the market, the more you'll have to pay in maintenance costs.
- **Realtor fees.** Realtors take care of the photography, marketing and listing of the property. They also meet clients first-hand and sell the property in person. Realtors typically charge 5% but many will accept 4% if you negotiate. If you skip realtors you'll have to sell the property yourself.

How To Calculate Your Net Profits

We use math to estimate the net profits once the property is sold. For the purpose of this demonstration we'll analyze one class-B property that we want to sell for $140,000.

Property price: $85,000

Renovation costs: $15,000

Buying closing costs: $1000

Selling closing costs: $5000

Taxes: $1000

The formula: $85,000 (property acquisition) + $22,000 (renovations + fees) = $33,000

NET PROFIT: $33,000

Once we take the final selling price of $140,000 and we subtract our total costs, we end up with a net profit of $33,000. The $33,000 figure is the net profit you're left with at the end of each sale. **Note**: There are separate buying costs at the start that include realtor fees on your end. There are also closing fees at the end that include your realtor fees and the buyer's realtor fees. If we estimate a moderate $15,000 budget for cosmetic upgrades, this amounts to $33,000 in pure profit.

The IRS taxes your flipping individually you'll have to pay at the end of each fiscal year, but it's impossible to calculate this in advance because if you aim to flip 3-4 properties a year, you'll be taxed on the combined profit from your flips. Most house flips are taxed under "capital gains" taxes which is a sub-category of income taxes that applies once someone sells an asset. For example, if a person inherits a $2M property and decides to sell it, the IRS will collect capital gains tax on the sale. If someone sells a business, capital gains taxes apply too. The same applies for your combined profits. House-flippers pay "short term capital gains" taxes for assets that they've held under a year. Short term capital gains taxes are almost 100% higher than those of long-term capital gains taxes (assets you've held for over a year). The lowest capital gains tax bracket is 10% for profits under $10,000 and it progressively increases up to 37% on profits over $500,000. Once you've calculated your total profits for the year, you can calculate your net profits based on the tax bracket and total profits.

Chapter 5 - It's All About Value

The 4 Best Value-Boosting Renovations

The magic number for renovating real estate is $40,000 - if you have $40,000 to spend you can install the highest quality bathrooms, kitchens and exterior renovations. You can revamp the home for half the price at $20,000 or even less - $10,000 if you're careful and do many things yourself. The two biggest value-boosters for a home are the kitchen and the bathroom. Those two alone can upgrade the value of a home by $50,000-100,000. We're talking big-revamps now! The big overhauls cost the most and can increase home value significantly. The kitchen is the heart of the home and making small adjustments to the kitchen area can significantly boost the value of the property. If this is your first flip, focus on the big 3: kitchen, bathroom and living room. There are many "small" upgrades which you can make such as paint jobs, light fixtures, landscaping, interior upgrades, etc, but most money in flipping is spent in the kitchen and bathroom. If you purchase a brand-new bathroom with the highest quality materials it can run up to $20,000 easily. There are ways to get that down by making small upgrades (which we'll distill below).

Let's talk numbers: The kitchen provides the highest ROI in terms of value. You will on average see a 3x return on your investment in the kitchen. **Example**: If you spend $5000 the buyer is going to think you spent $15,000. The bathroom also has a huge multiplier. For each $5000 you spend on a bathroom, the buyer will think you spent $10,000. If you spend $20,000 on a bathroom the buyer will think you spent $40,000. Paint has a significant impact on ROI. On average, for each gallon of paint you spend on the home you will see a return of $1000. If you spend 10 gallons of paint you will a property value increase of $10,000. There are small improvements that can be made to the home such as security upgrades/smart devices, but the bulk of your budget will be allocated on the big upgrades. We'll show you how to spend small on those big upgrades and which kitchen/bathroom updates provide the highest ROI (ones that you can upgrade on a budget). We focus upgrades based on market demand, and the following upgrades are the most sought-after on the US real-estate market.

Bearing that in mind, the following 4 upgrades will increase the value of your property significantly:

Renovation #1) The Kitchen

The phrase "The Kitchen is the heart of the home" holds true - you must start your renovations with the kitchen. The main cosmetic upgrades you must make are inside the kitchen - if the counters are too outdated you have to replace them or paint them. People will analyze the state of the kitchen first to get a sense for the state of the rest of the house. Families spend a lot of time in the kitchen and buyers have very specific demands as to the amenities they require. Most people don't wish to fiddle with small purchases and prefer everything delivered turnkey, which is why they'll expect you to present them with a fully remodeled kitchen. The kitchen has to have the newest appliances such as fridges, trendy stoves, double-sinks, kitchen islands, microwaves, dishwashers and more. The more "modern" your appliances the faster the property will sell. You want the average buyer to imagine themselves waking up and having coffee on that kitchen countertop. The kitchen can get very expensive as smart appliances alone could run up to thousands of dollars. Turkey kitchens are also more expensive than individually purchasing appliances. This is why we focus on small improvements that have a big impact on kitchen renovations.

- **Kitchen Upgrade #1:** Double Sink
- **Average Cost:** $100-$50

Replace the sink with a double-sink: This is a cheap, popular upgrade that is viewed as an essential by the majority of Millennial and younger generation buyers. Surveys show that middle-income buyers require a double-sink as a necessity and they need enough space to store all their large pots and pens. The deeper the sink, the more space they have, the better. Aim for a sink that is going to contain splashes and allow enough space to contain multiple large pots, pans and dishes. The sink doesn't have to be extravagant: It can be a simple, functional and easy to clean sink. Purchase a sink with a modern touch to add to the "premium" feeling of the kitchen.

- **Kitchen Upgrade #2**: Kitchen Island
- **Average Cost**: $200-500

The most sought-after feature in kitchens is a kitchen-island. Fortunately, kitchen islands are affordable upgrades and can be found for under $500. Almost 80% of all new home-buyers require a kitchen island as an essential, and the island is synonymous with American kitchen culture. Families require a space where they can carve their groceries, prepare coffee/smoothies, entertain guests, talk in the morning and store their essentials. The kitchen sink provides additional eating space to the main table (very desirable kitchen feature!) and it adds storage space separate from the main fridge. The kitchen will center around the kitchen island and you might want to allocate more of your budget on the island because it sets the tone of the kitchen. Most kitchen islands are "pre made" which means they can fit into all empty spaces.

- **Kitchen Upgrade #3**: Paint Cabinets
- **Average cost**: $30-50/gallon of paint

Does your property come with old kitchen cabinets? Replacement cabinets are affordable but what's more affordable is painting them! You can reshape the vibe of a kitchen by re-painting the rusty old cabinets with a simple brush in under 1 hour. If the room feels too "small" and "dark" this can be a result of old dark cabinets that need refreshing. The quickest cure for a dark room is to liven up the colors by opening it up with light colors. We recommend neutral white or grey paint that will create the illusion of space and brighten the room. These neutral colors are welcoming and paint only costs $30-50/gallon. The effects on the kitchen will be significant and you can save money instead of replacing the cabinets.

Renovation #2) The Bathroom

The bathroom provides ROI on a 2x average basis: If you invest $15,000 in a bathroom the buyer will think you invested $30,000. For example, you can install new three-light fixtures for under $100 that give the bathroom a five-star hotel look and the buyer will think you invested thousands in the light fixtures of the bathroom. A ready "turnkey" bathroom can cost tens of thousands of dollars. To get around that, you have to remodel the most important essentials of a bathroom such as shower stall, fixtures, toilets, vanity and shower heads. These upgrades are cheap and cost a few hundred dollars at most. If you combine the most essential upgrades, you can modernize the bathroom without overspending. Concentrate on the details: Purchase modern upgrades that give the bathroom a fresh start. The following are the most essential upgrades that increase the outlook of a bathroom significantly:

> **Bathroom Upgrade #1**: Fixtures (handles, faucets, and shower heads)
> **Average Cost**: $100-$200

The main cosmetic upgrades in the bathroom are the fixtures - if you replace fixtures with modern fixtures it gives the bathroom a shiny and clean feeling, almost as if you bought a turnkey bathroom. This boosts the appeal of the bathroom significantly. Star overhauling the bathroom by installing new shower-heads or faucets. If you have old rusty shower heads with visible tear and wear, this is very bad for the image of the bathroom. New shower-heads can be replaced for under $100. Dismantle the old flickering light at the ceiling and purchase new three-way light fixtures that are modern and illuminate the room in bright LED light. For the sink faucet, purchase one with a new brushed nickel finish that adds style. Purchase a nickel showerhead for efficient water usage and shininess. Consider a new light fixture above the vanity which will usually cost under $100.

- **Bathroom Upgrade #2**: Toilets
- **Average Cost**: $100-200 (+ $300 for installation).

The main upgrade new clients will appreciate in a bathroom is a new toilet! Most time in the bathroom is spent on the toilet and clients don't want to use toilets that were used by other people for years. You want to purchase and replace the toilet with a spanking new one. Many outdated toilets also have bowls that leak gallons of water at night without your knowledge which makes this an essential upgrade. Fortunately toilets can cost as low as $100 and the most expensive ones are below $300. Installation costs are higher than the toilet itself, but you can find deals in places like Home Depot which installs toilets for under $300. Many new toilets come with different color options and flush the water in a powerful way. If you want to upgrade the toilet consider adding a bidet which many clients will appreciate.

- **Bathroom Upgrade #3**: Vanity
- **Average Cost**: $200-$500

The vanity is a bathroom essential of similar significance to the toilet because the vanity is a part of our morning and night routines! The vanity is the first thing we use in the morning and the last thing we use at night. We place our essentials in the vanity and you want to make sure the vanity is something your new clients would want to use daily. The vanity can bring significant returns on the bathroom. Focus on the details to see if you can repaint or fix the current vanity before you purchase a new one. If you repaint the vanity use neutral colors such as white, grey or beige. A new vanity can cost up to $500 depending on the materials used and the size of the vanity. Your vanity must have a new modern countertop, a sink, faucet with decent height and a clean finish. If there is an outdated mirror you can replace it with a cheap one, expanding the space in the room and giving it a sleeker, modern look.

Renovation #3) Flooring/Carpeting

➢ **Average Cost**: $6-10/sq ft.

The floor in the living room is one of the "big 3" upgrades aside from kitchen and bathroom. If you upgrade the living room floor you can add significant value to the resell price of your property - everyone wants a new floor. The average cost of a new floor is $6-10 per square foot. This means that the floor of a large living room can be completely replaced for under $1000. However, it doesn't mean that you can't go lower. There are certain materials that can go for as little as $3/square foot. If you opt for the most luxurious materials you will pay up to $20/square foot. This depends on the total makeover and/or impression you're trying to create on buyers. The quality of the floor is one of the first things they'll notice aside from the paint-job. Floors are something you can't do on your own, however, labor costs are not exuberant and the average 300 sq. ft living room can be replaced for $1000 not including materials. The floor is a huge upgrade for a new house because the owners won't have to bother getting it replaced themselves. You can completely reshape the vibe of the living room: If you purchase black-colored floors, the home will have a more modern and neutral look. To complete the flooring upgrades purchase a modern carpet that your new buyers will love. As a rule of thumb, copy floors in your neighborhood.

Renovation #4) Install Patio/Deck

➢ **Average Cost**: $2000-4000/patio

The biggest value-booster in certain states is installing a patio or a deck. Does the home have a back yard where you can install an additional patio to lay down chairs and relax? Building one can boost the property value significantly. People who love to entertain in warmer states will find this a plus because they can enjoy an outdoor space to relax, cook, eat, drink, play with children and hold events. There is the possibility to extend the patio to the pool area if there is a pool in the back of the house.

The patio converts the house into a "summer oasis" where the owners can host parties and bring guests over. Patios are a great investment because they enable future owners to create long-lasting memories and many owners would pay more if they have a good patio. The installation cost is not exuberant: The average concrete patio costs $700 in materials, and once labor costs/contractors are added it amounts to $2000-4000 per patio. A small investment of this kind can re-shape the vibe of the property; however, in colder states this is not desirable as there's less time to enjoy the outdoors.

Curb Appeal: What It Is & How to Do It Right

Curb appeal is a term used to describe the first impression a person gets when they drive past a house. Drive past a row of house - what's the first thing you think about them? Do you think "That's a nice house" or "That house sucks" when you drive past them? Your reaction is determined by the curb appeal! If the house has a good curb appeal, you will have a good first impression. If the house has a bad curb appeal, you have a bad first impression. Curb appeal is determined by the exterior: the paint job of the house, the light fixtures, the lawn, patio, cars parked and other minor details. The curb appeal translates to pictures taken online as people open houses based on the state of the exterior - if they like the exterior they want to see the interior. In essence, your house could be falling apart on the inside but if the exterior looks maintained it will have a good curb appeal for passer-bys. To improve curb appeal, we focus on exterior decorations, re-painting, landscaping and general maintenance.

The HOA (Homeowners Association) focuses on curb appeal by hiring contractors who power-wash and maintain public driveways. This way each home in the neighborhood is maintained and the neighborhood can maintain high property values. If a resident of an HOA community refuses to pay they can be fined as they signed a legal document to own in a community with mandatory maintenance. Home-owners and building contractors use multiple ways to increase the curb appeal which makes the house more valuable. Buyers want to see a property in good shape before they sign a mortgage: They want to feel "at home". To create this, you must make upgrades that will create a homely feeling for the new buyers.

Curb appeal is also the reaction your neighbors have once they walk/drive past your house - it's not only appeal to buyers. Example: If you walk past a neighbors property and think "Wow his outdoor lighting enhances the landscaping" you reinforce the positive impressions you have of their home. Children playing can also be a sign of high curb appeal as children only play in front lawns that have lush green turf ideal for sport activities. Before you try to sell a property, you want to maximize the curb appeal it has because this will create good first impressions for future buyers. You want to assign a certain percentage of your renovation budget to essentials that increase curb appeal and make the house appealing to future buyers. Upgrades that boost curb appeal significantly are exterior paint and light fixtures: Curb-appeal essentials can be upgraded for a few thousand dollars and the increase in home value will be significant.

Curb Appeal Booster #1: Exterior Paint

> **Average Cost**: $100-200/2-3 gallons (+$20 for brushes!)

The paint job gives the impression that the home is maintained and in good shape. Cosmetic upgrades on the home increase home value significantly and the most essential of such is the exterior paint. Re-painting your home will attract buyers and increase the value of your property. New paint will not only renew the look of the property but it will keep it safe against the elements. For each gallon you put in the exterior paint-job, you will see a return of $1000/gallon.

Note: Painting the exterior is ideal for homes that are in decent shape and could use a renewal - it won't do much for a decaying property that requires new walls and insulation.

Contractors might increase the price of a paint job by a margin of 2-3x. The best way to save money on an exterior paint is to paint it yourself. Bring your dad or brother in law and paint the home yourselves - it should take you no longer than 2 days to paint a 2000 sq foot home exterior. If you're on a budget this is a huge money-saver. Focus on covering all the blemishes and camouflage any peeling spots. Make sure the color matches the exteriors of other homes in the area. On average, you will spend $30-50 per gallon of paint. This means that to cover the exterior you will need only $100-200 depending on the size of the house. Equipment such as brushes and supplies will add up to only $20-30. Then you're on to painting! The paint will boost your curb appeal and it should be done at the end of your renovations, to remain fresh for the realtor showings and "open houses" that sell the property.

Curb Appeal Booster #2: Smart LEDs

➢ **Average Cost**: $100-200

Exterior light can increase curb appeal and deter criminals - this is a win-win. Exterior light is one of the key essential features that new home buyers look for and newer "smart" lights are desirable as they illuminate the front entire patio/driveway and can be activated using motion sensors. New lights are energy-efficient and can light up the front of your house for the entire night without costing you a fortune. For under $300 in light fixtures, you can convert cold patios into warm and welcoming spaces that create an evening ambience for guests and showings.

The realtor can show your property at night and display a warm atmosphere that will sell the house. LED lights are very desirable as they build a cozy atmosphere and keep the home safe. Installation is prompt and new fixtures can be attached and installed in under an hour. To finalize your light upgrades, purchase motion-sensor activated headlights that you place above the garage. If you want to maximize your curb appeal at night, consider purchasing waterproof solar fairy LED's that you can lay out all along your front yard fence that will create a homely feeling for passerby's.

Small Updates for a Significantly More Desirable Home

Congratulations – you've made the big upgrades! Let's assume you've spent $5000 on a kitchen and $10,000 on a bathroom - each property has unique requirements based on the state of the interior. The property you buy might have had a bad bathroom with a new(ish) kitchen. In that case you assign 50% of your renovation budget on the bathroom and make small upgrades on the rest. The important factor is to "even out" the home with equal standards throughout each room. You don't want to have a smart kitchen and then a 60s decrepit bathroom in the next room. Congratulations – you've made the big upgrades! What happens once you've done all the big renovations and you're ready to sell on the market? There are numerous small upgrades that cost under $1000 which can help secure and "smartify" the home. Buyers will purchase a home branded as "smart" even if it's more expensive than a regular home in good shape. The surprising fact is that most security gadgets and smart features cost only a few hundred dollars. In theory, you could equip the home with the latest technology by spending almost no money.

We focus on 3 minor upgrades: security systems, smart tech and landscaping. Those upgrades provide the highest bang for your buck and ROI on homes. Statistically the US has a burglary every 18 seconds and it makes sense to equip your property with the latest security tech. Most "all in one" security systems come with cameras, motion sensors and Smartphone app compatibility. We also recommend installing smart thermostats that help buyers configure the temperature in their home. Finally we recommend minor landscaping upgrades that can increase the curb appeal of the home. The following minor upgrades will significantly impact the value of your property:

Value Upgrade #1) Wireless Security Systems

> **Average Cost**: $50-$200

Security systems operate wirelessly via WiFi and can be installed in under an hour: Most home-security packages you purchase on Amazon can provide you with multiple security cameras to cover every angle and interior of the house. You can install a camera on the front of the house, the living room, the back porch and any areas you desire. The camera's motion sensors will pick up on movement and send you signals to your smartphone while you're at work using WiFi. Advanced camera systems can also identify smoke and prevent house fires. If you spend a few more bucks, you can purchase a camera that has night vision to protect you from burglars at night (or even help capture criminals if your neighbor's home is burglarized by monitoring the immediate neighborhood!). Many security cameras have backup batteries that help them operate while you're on vacation or in case of a power outage.

The average smart security camera costs $50-100, but a full set can be had in the $200-300 range that includes multiple cameras for 24/7 security. Make sure the camera you purchase is DYI (do it yourself) and allows you to install the system on your own. To save money, purchase security systems that don't have monthly subscription systems. Many manufacturers hook clients on monthly fees to use their security software - find ones that come without monthly charges. Security systems will enhance the safety of the home and help sell it easier.

Value Upgrade #2) Smart Thermostat

> **Average Cost**: $200-400

Research shows that one of the cheapest and fastest ways to smartification and increasing property value is to install a high-tech thermostat. The benefits of smart thermostats are numerous: They save time, conserve energy, adapt to your lifestyle and help you configure the temperate of your home. The best all-around thermostats you can find on Amazon will analyze the work patterns of the residents and use that to lower the heat when they're at work and turn it up once they're back home. Thermostats take under an hour to install and can be done DYI: They have low maintenance and work in conjunction with smartphone apps. The best systems cost in the range of $200-400, depending on the coverage. This feature will sell a home fast and it can be one of the main talking points once you show it off to buyers.

Value Upgrade #3) Landscaping

> **Average Cost**: $50-$100

Lawns increase property value and many HOA communities enforce laws for lawn maintenance, fining residents who fail to adhere to the guidelines. The lawn has to be green and well-maintained with no yellow patches or ground holes. Research shows that in house-flipping adequate maintenance of the lawn recovers 100% of the initial renovation costs at the time of the sale and can boost the home value by 5-10%. To maintain a lawn you can hire a contractor or do it yourself (best money saver!). Go to the hardware store and purchase hedge trimmers and a lawn mower that you can use to start working.

If you want to upgrade your lawn, plant primrose bushes or use pavers to line the driveway. This will boost the curb appeal of your home significantly, and primrose bushes are very easy to maintain. If you have any yellow spots you can get paint and fill them in before you start taking pictures or showing them to buyers. These changes take a few hours of work at most and they have a serious impact on the perception and value of your property.

Value Upgrade #4) New Ceiling Fans

> **Average Cost**: $100/fan + $100 for installation

Real estate institute research shows that ceiling fans are loved by buyers of all income brackets - if the home lacks ceiling fans you can add them for less than $100 each. The ceiling fan adds extra lighting and comfort. If your property is in a warm state, you absolutely need ceiling fans. There should be a ceiling fan in the living room and each bedroom: That will create a homely feeling as you navigate the house. If you're unsure as to whether ceiling fans are practical in your area, analyze the comps or visit properties nearby and consult with the residents. The ceiling fan design has to be minimalistic and not "overwhelm" the room you're renovating. The go-to ceiling fan design is pure matte black with wooden blades.

Green Improvements that Instantly Increase a Home's Value

Energy efficiency is a term for upgrading the house with equipment that preserves heat or keep the home cool, saving on costs. Energy efficiency does not have to be expensive! Yes, a solar panel installation will cost $14,000 on average but mere upgrades such as replacing the windows can cost only $2000-3000 a house. Energy-efficiency multiplies each dollar you put in the property by a multiplier of 2x. If you invest $5000 in energy-efficiency you will get $10,000 back. If you update the energy-efficiency of a house you can convince your future buyers that they're buying an energy-efficient house using hard numbers. In states like California all new developments have to have solar panels or they are not eligible for a building permit. If you want to upgrade the home for complete energy efficiency without relying on the public grid, you can do this for as little as $15,000. The price will depend upon the quality of the panels and the size of the home. Similar rules apply for making small upgrades such as the insulation or window replacement.

Simple upgrades can make the home green and boost energy-efficiency. **Example**: Replacing age-old windows with new double-paned windows can reduce cooling bills by 15% and save the residents $500 a year in utility costs. LED lights are ultra-conservative on energy and the electricity is virtually for free once you switch to LED fixtures. If you replace each light in the house with a new LED fixture, you can explain how the lighting system of the house is built for longevity and how they'll save on electricity bills in the long run. Seek out government-funded energy efficiency initiatives in your state, as many states will subsidize the purchases of energy-efficient windows, lights and solar panels. The following are the most popular upgrades that you can install on virtually every home in the US:

Green Upgrade #1) Energy-Efficient Windows

Average Cost: $150-300/window

Windows have impact on heat penetration that comes in and leaves the property - almost as much as insulation. If the insulation of the property is on par with modern standards, the windows have to be brought up to par to withstand every climate. The weather is getting more extreme in both the summer and the winter: The summers are hotter and the winters are colder. The newest windows that have an "Energy Star" rating are desirable and considered environmentally-friendly. Windows will boost the property value by a multiplier of 2x similar to solar panels. Vinyl windows are the go-to for flippers because they are easy to install/maintain, durable, energy-efficient and environmentally friendly. The average price per window is $150-300 depending on the size of the window. If the home has 20 windows, you can replace each window in the house for as low as $3000.

Green Upgrade #2) Solar Panels

Average Cost: $10,000-15,000/house

Solar panels are the ultimate upgrade in green energy - certain states are now mandating that to get a building permit each new construction has to have solar panels. They're a go-to upgrade for all warm states because the year-round sunshine can provide easy energy-efficiency and the investment pays off in as little as 10 years. Solar panels help harvest the energy of the natural environment. To equip a house for 100% energy-efficiency using solar panels, you will spend on average $10,000-15,000 for the whole house. The total costs may exceed $20,000 in some states but every state subsidizes solar panels which brings down the average significantly. There are many tax rebates and credits you can apply on the federal and state levels once you switch to solar panels. This will be considered a major upgrade for all homes and make it an easy sell because the new buyer doesn't have to haggle installing them. The average solar system with 20 solar panels will only take 1-3 days to install. This is an easy upgrade if you have the budget and you deem it necessary in your state.

Each dollar that you invest in energy-efficiency will provide a magnificent return once it's time to sell! The only downside is that this is not a priority for low-cost flips. It's also not practical for cold states. Analyze how much energy the property you're purchasing consumes currently and how much it will save after the energy-efficient upgrades are made. There are upgrades for every budget and for maximum energy-efficiency the average person won't have to exceed $20,000 - that includes all solar panel installations, LED upgrades, insulation and window upgrades.

Chapter 6 - Making It Shine

Putting Together the Rehab Dream Team

You've financed the deals, you signed the checks, you bought your first house! Congratulations! The next step is to assemble your "Dream Team" of contractors, lawyers and real-estate professionals. Who would ever need a lawyer, you might ask? Every financial transaction you make will have to be documented by lawyers who can ensure you don't end up with lawsuits and your accountant/CPA will take care of your taxes to keep you safe from Uncle Sam. Contractors can make our break your deal, and assembling a team of contractors is essential - there are many ways to save money on contractors which we'll distill below.

In real estate you can hire "General Contractors/GC's" who do all the rehab work at once (re-structuring, painting, flooring, roofing) or you can hire sub-contractors for each one of those individual professions. It's easy to find each one of those professionals - they're all connected and working together. Once you have a friend who is in real estate, you can get referrals to contractors in your area. There is also the possibility to look them up online, as many contractors operate in their immediate area exclusively. It's very rare to meet a construction crew in California that came all the way from Florida. Flipping is done the old-fashioned way on a community basis.

Your "Dream Team" has to be assembled based on an essential and non-essential basis. Some people are absolutely essential: Lawyers and contractors. Other people are not essential: Realtors and architects. The rules change: Contractors can be non-essential if you're familiar with construction work and can carry out repairs yourself. However, for most flippers trade work is out of the equation because it requires a lot of expertise and it's risky to do jobs you're not familiar with (for safety and legal reasons). Don't make mistakes and end up with a lawsuit at start of your flip - hire an attorney to look at each end of the sale, the purchase documents and the closing sale. There's a reason some lawyers charge $500/hour - once they've overlooked the details to your sale in that single hour, they can estimate mistakes that might cost you thousands of dollars in long-term costs or a potential lawsuit.

Remember: You hire professionals at every stage of the flip. Your "Dream Team" won't work with you for the duration of the whole flip.

At the start you will need to mobilize a lawyer to look over your avulsion and financing papers. Once you've had a lawyer's seal of approval, you can proceed with the purchase. You will then need to decide if you want to hire a 'General Contractor' who will carry out all repairs for you at a negotiated cost, or hire sub-contractors for the individual branch of work you need done. We'll teach you how to pick out the best contractors for the lowest price. If this is your first project, you're best off hiring a GC in your area who will carry out all repairs for once. Accountants are necessary after each flip to analyze the financial documents and estimate your taxes before and after. Landscapers and handymen might be needed depending on the state of your property. Architects are only necessary if you plan to tear down or add space which requires special drawings and permits. Finally, realtors can help you sell a home and do all the work for you for a commission. The following 2 categories highlight which people you will need to hire to get started in house-flipping:

Essential Professionals

1) Lawyers.

The lawyer is the most essential piece of the puzzle: They draw up the contractors before you purchase a property and settle the sale once you've sold a property. They can identify flaws in your contracts that you never knew existed and/or could lead to lawsuits. To be safe, always pick a lawyer who specializes in real estate rather than general practice. Real estate lawyers in your area will be familiar with local zoning laws and they're especially useful if you plan to add or remove space to get permits for construction. Lawyers will inform you if your flipping practices are compliant with local laws. Lawyers charge high hourly rates because their job demands a lot of attention to detail and they'll have to review the deal first, in addition to being present at inspections and closings. Many lawyers starting out will agree to work with as little as $100-150 an hour because they're trying to make a name for themselves. The average for an established real estate lawyer can be $200-300/h and you only need them for a few hours each month. Some lawyers will agree to work for a $1000-2000 advance payment on each flip no matter how many hours they work.

> **Average Cost**: $150-300/h

2) Accountants.

Accountants/CPAs are an essential piece of the puzzle that work alongside lawyers. The accountant or "CPA" is in charge of all your financial details and keeps track of the taxes you must pay and advise you on tax rebates that you can write off. If you hire a CPA you will find out which items you've invested in can be "written off" on your tax records. For example, if you purchase solar panels a CPA can tell you how much you can write off for that purchase in your state and save you money. They can help you establish your business structure file all your taxes for you and ensure your financial documents are in order for flippers who do multiple flips per year. Most CPAs will require 1 or 2 hours a month to handle your documents and offer "monthly plans" or you can pay a yearly $1000-2000 to a CPA to have them on call and file your documents on April 15th.

> **Average Cost**: $500-1000/year

3) General Contractors/GCs.

The most essential piece of the puzzle once your legal documents are settled are the people who actually make renovations happen! General Contractors or "GC's" in short can oversee your entire rehabilitation effort and a single person hires their own qualified professionals who can repair a property swiftly without involving multiple crews. General Contractors specialize in all trades at once and their crews are experienced with all renovation types. They can renovate the kitchen, bathroom, floors, tear down/add space, or anything required to complete your renovation. This decreases the potential for error as a single crew is in charge of the renovations and you don't have to deal with a set of sub-contractors, one of which might turn out unreliable. Once you've found a General Contractor you only have to worry about the sale of the property because they will carry out all renovations without you lifting a finger. General Contractors don't charge hourly fees but they settle on a fixed renovation cost based on your budget and their estimated costs: They will give you a bid and if you agree on the bid they will carry out all renovations within that budget range.

> **Average Cost**: Negotiated

Non-Essential Professionals

1) Realtors.

Most houses in the US are sold through realtors: These are licensed professionals who specialize in the sales process of a house. They handle all the listing/marketing, presentations, showings and they ensure a final sale on the property. Realtors charge significant commissions for their work and some realtors can take 6% on the sale of a house (3% for the buyer's realtor and 3% for the seller's realtor). However, their knowledge as to the market data for neighborhoods, sales tactics and sweat equity compensate for their commissions (which are negotiable). Realtors are paid by sellers/flippers and if you choose to hire a realtor you will have to pay them out of pocket based on a pre-agreed fee. Realtors are useful for people trying to fix multiple properties who don't have time to deal with buyers first-hand.

> **Average Cost**: 6%/sale

2) Landscapers.

Landscapers boost the curb appeal of the property and make the exterior look more appealing to buyers. Landscapers are usually hired on an "as-needed" basis as they're only necessary once the final repairs are carried out and you need to put the finishing touches on a property. Basic landscaping such as lawn mowing is something you can do on your own, but landscapers can help re-grow dead grass or cover up yellow patches. They can also position plants, trim your existing garden and ensure everything is adequate and ready to sell. The average landscaper will work for $60/h not including materials.

➢ **Average Cost**: $50-70/h

3) Architects.

Architects are non-essential in "house-flipping" because architects design the new – you're buying and selling existing properties. Architects specialize in drawing up and estimating structural size to ensure the building will be structurally-sound and their work is required before a construction crew goes to work. However, once the house is built architects are only required once you need to remove a room/change the structure or add more space on the exterior. Architects are also hired on an "as-needed" basis and they can be quite costly with an average of $100/h. Many architects will agree to work for a fixed fee and are open to negotiations.

➢ **Average Cost**: $70-150/h

4) Handymen.

Handymen are general workers who give you a hand (as the name implies) and technically a handyman could be your father, brother in law, wife, or the student who lives down the street and need a few extra dollars. Handymen will be essential because many times you need someone to help you paint the rooms, patch up holes, install new cabinets and change the interior of the home. A handyman doesn't need to be licensed as they'll mostly be assisting with regular work. Handymen can be hired on the internet and many have extensive experience in construction and can help you with all your needs. The average you should pay a handyman is $30-60/h and try to get as much done in those hours to get the most bang for your buck.

> **Average Cost**: $30-60/h

5) Assistants.

Once you've made it big in flipping and you're starting to make 5-10 flips a year, hire a personal assistant who can be present on location with you and help you with your daily activities. This must be someone you can trust and it's recommended to hire inside your family to not get tricked. An assistant is a person who will be with you at the job site, dealing with contractors, meeting financiers, closing deals and delivering your papers to lawyers. An assistant can take 50% of the work load off your back. This is why it's better to hire inside the family – if their livelihood depends on the job, they'll be much more motivated.

> **Average Cost**: Negotiated

How do you find the general contractors, lawyers and individual sub-contractors? The answer: Classified ads in your local area. In most cases you can pop-over at a construction site and ask the workers to see the "boss" and have a chat with them: They will give you referrals for general contractors in your city. Make sure that the contractors you hire are licensed and experienced - they must have the know-how to carry out the professional tasks you hire them to. This will save you money because you won't have to pay for the same job twice.

How to Find the Best Contractor for Your Property

House-flipping is a team effort and all experienced house-flippers hire contractors at a certain point. There are no rules written in stone: One could purchase a house, renovate it themselves, and sell the house on their own - bypassing all contractor and realtor fees. However, in practice it's better to hire professionals who will carry out a high-quality job and allow you the time to focus on multiple projects at once. Hiring contractors is the hardest piece of the puzzle as you'll have to do almost as much research as you did buying a house. The contractors will oversee all your rehabilitations and renovations and a General Contractor can provide the material, labor, equipment/tools and render all those services at once.

General Contractors Vs Sub-Contractors

House-flipping schools of thought differ on the whole "debate" of GC's vs sub-contractors. GC's are known to get things done at once, but sub-contractors are deemed economical as they're only hired on an "as needed" basis. A good GC can carry out all renovations at a fixed price without over-charging you for unexpected surprises. General contractors are better for flippers who want to take a more "hands off" approach and focus on financing multiple projects at once. They save time and allow a flipper to focus on securing more finances, finding buyers and locating new properties. However, sub-contractors are better if you know your property only requires one or two repairs and you can hire sub-contractors for those repairs specifically.

GC's are have "crews" that can dispatch to your location and rehabilitate the property in a single swing. The boss will have a crew of guys who he manages under his wing and they will assign work based on the needs of your property. The benefit for flippers is that you're only paying one contractor for the whole renovation. This way you don't have to seek out and hire individual sub-contractors every time you need a room painted, a bathroom sink installed or a floor changed - the GC takes care of all that for you! General Contractors can be quite large and many of them work on multiple properties at once, managing hundreds of workers. They can switch employees between job sites. If one carpenter finishes a job at a certain property and your property requires a carpenter, they can be dispatched to your location.

To finalize the debate, ask yourself the following question: "Are my changes cosmetic?". If the changes you need on your property are cosmetic, you don't need a GC. If the renovations are focused on kitchen improvements (replacing sinks, appliances, countertops, kitchen islands, etc), bathroom renovations (toilets, counters, mirrors, sinks), paint-jobs (interior and exterior), floor changes (new floors) and landscaping - you can make these 'cosmetic' upgrades on your own or with the help of a few sub-contractors. If the renovations are larger and they require work on the foundation of the property and/or adding space you should hire a General Contractor.

General Contractors can work with architects and they can carry out demolitions/add-ons depending on what you need - they will help you get the drawings in order and get the building permits you need from your municipality before you build. Significant changes such as adding square footage, tearing down walls, adding rooms, changing roofs, foundation changes, etc, - those will all require General Contractors.

How To Discover Contractors

The real estate industry is "old fashioned" and most connections in the business are made through real-life interaction with contractors and referrals. You'll have to attend conferences, shake hands, call people and/or visit construction sites.

➤ **Referrals**. Join your local real estate investment group or attend conferences where you can meet people. A referral can be given by virtually any person: Fellow entrepreneur, flipping competitors, or even your neighbor. Ask real estate investors in the area who they've worked with and who they can vouch for. In many cases, you'll hear the same few names as usually big firms dominate a certain area. Inquire as to the efficiency and budgeting of the contractor (especially when hiring a GC). Ask if they finished the projects on time as delays can cost you thousands of dollars and ask about the total budget. If possible, visit properties that the GCs have worked on in the past.

➤ **Visit construction sites**. If you spot a construction site on your daily commute, park your car and talk to the workers there or talk to the boss if he's present on the job site. Flag down a worker and make a simple introduction. Say that you're going to need repairs and ask them how you can get in touch with their company for potential work. They will likely put you in touch with their boss and hand you a card - therefore allowing you to research them online and analyzing their past work.

➢ **Visit "building departments"**. Each city has a local "building department" that keeps track of which firms were granted construction permits - this way you can analyze firms that are operational at the moment and currently engaged with projects. It's possible that a firm went out of business if they were granted permits 3 years ago and you need recent data from the last 3-6 months. All General Contractors have to file for permits to do certain kind of work (mostly adding/removing rooms) and those have to pass inspections by city agents. If a contractor was granted a permit, that means they're doing top-notch work that complies with local building codes. The building department can provide you with information for all contractors currently operational in your area.

➢ **Online research**. Start with Google and look up "General Contractor + [Your City]" top find a list of General Contractors operational in your area. It's not recommend to opt for the first listings because they are the most popular and will charge the highest fees. Seek out lesser-known contractors that have a good reputation. An excellent source for local contractors and sub-contractors is Craigslist - advertising there is free and it's easy to discover many working contractors. Join real estate forums where flippers share insider information and can help you with any problem you stumble across.

Hire Licensed Contractors

Only hire licensed and insured contactors – GC's are not handymen that you can hire on the go. Your contractor has to be licensed in order to operate in your state and they must have insurance in case something goes wrong on your property (so you don't pay out of pocket!). A contractor should help you come up with a price sheet that will include prices by the sq. ft for things such as paint, floors, carpets. The sheet should include items that need replacing such as windows, fixtures, blinds, doors, appliances and more. Essential items have to be "pre agreed" therefore the contractor doesn't hit you by surprise with extra charges. Many times you won't work with the same contractors for longer than 6 months or a year - contractors come and go. Inform your contractors as to the exact amount you can afford to make sure their work is within the scope of your budget.

Pro Tip: You only negotiate with your contractor the first flip. Take your time to agree on the lowest price possible. If the contractor is successful, the next jobs won't require negotiations as you've already agreed on pre-set prices.

How To Pay Contractors

There are two ways to pay contractors: By-weekly or based on the work they've completed. Certain jobs might take longer than you initially planned for, and you should only pay based on the results. Refuse to pay contractors in advance because they might take your money and not complete the job. Make sure to compensate your contractors for each milestone completed. If they've finished the kitchen - pay them for the kitchen. If the renovate the whole house - pay them for the whole house. Never pay in advance for work that hasn't been completed.

Make It Shine While Minimizing Costs

You're ready to call contractors and negotiate prices: How do you sniff out which ones are going to do the most kick-ass job at the lowest price? How do you know if a contractor will over-charge you or give you a fair deal? In many cases there is nothing you can do about a bad contractor once you've agreed on a price - this is why you must cross-reference multiple contractors in advance. There are many methods you can employ to save money in advance such as investing in power-tools that you won't have to rent out for the job. If you have the tools necessary, you can watch tutorials and try to carry out the job yourself. Even if you hire contractors, they'll appreciate having an extra set of tools by their side. Aside from investing in power tools (important for all renovations!) you can hire dumpsters for the waste that will accumulate on the property and avoid the surcharges of a contractor bringing one. The following are the best ways to make your property shine without spending a lot of money:

Golden Rule #1) Call 3 Contractors At Once

You're new to the business - if you hire the GC you come across there's a 50% chance you'll make a profit and 50% chance they'll overcharge you and send your investment in a downward spiral. How do you decide which contractor to go for? Make them enter a bid war! Gather a list of the most appropriate contractors in your area based on their rate and call them each individually. Describe your property and needs to the contractor and once they have your details ask the magical question: "What is your bid?". The contractor will give you an approximate estimate based on the materials needed, the extent of the job and the time necessary. They may even reveal certain details about the job that you didn't realize were necessary. Most contractors bid by the square foot. For example, a flooring contractor will tell you how much the floor costs per square foot and the labor for each square foot assembled. Once you have 3 separate bids, you can make your decision based on which one is the lowest or best for the job. Calls are a real eye-opener because you can sense how truthful and knowledgeable the contractor is about the job! The more personal your interaction, the more you'll be aware of what to expect from that contractor.

Golden Rule #2) Ask About Fee Structure

If you have a general idea for the costs, you have to inquire as to the potential fee structure to understand if the contractor is familiar with house-flipping and the repeat business you can provide them. When you get in touch with a contractor ask them how much they would charge to complete a job for a 1500 sq. foot house. Let's say you need a full paint-job for the house that includes the ceilings. A "good" price for a paint-job of that kind would be $1/sq. foot or around $1500 total for the job. The contractor will quote you based on the size of the house and if they quote double ($3000) you know they aren't the right contractor for you. Which is good news! Because it means you're ready to move on to a more eligible contractor who knows the value of repeat business. Always inquire in terms of square footage: If you haven't bought a house yet, make up a random number such as 1500 square feet or 2000 square feet.

Money Saver #1) Free Planning

The best part about large department stores where you purchase merchandise is that many times they provide "free planning". This will save you copious amounts of money on interior designers once you're ready to renovate the big 3: The bathroom, bedrooms and living room. Most home-improvement stores you drive past will have designers on hand who will help you draft up a free plan if you purchase your materials from the store. Make sure the store you're buying from has a free "design consultation". In essence, you're getting a free interior designer who will re-design the shape of your interior at no charge.

Money Saver #2) Buying Overstocked Materials

Visit the local building-supply store or a large hardware store that supplies a huge chunk of the hardware market in your area. Those stores usually have "overstocked" merchandise that is sitting around in their back isles. Once you're at the store ask to talk to the manger and then inquire as to items you need that are in their inventory. It's possible to purchase overstocked items at discounts of up to 50% if you only engage with the manager. This is essential once you're buying power tools for your first flip.

Money Saver #3) Purchase Power Tools

You only have to do this once! The average power-tool costs between $50-100 and you can purchase a full set of power tools that you can use on your jobs for as little as $1000 - you will be using these power tools for years. When you pay a contractor, you're paying for their tools indirectly. If you rent tools, you have to return them and you can't re-use them on future jobs. Once you buy your own tools, they're there forever! If you prefer to save on your renovations and you're a DYI type, the following are the most essential tools you'll need for flipping job:

- **Power Washer** (to clean the decks/siding/exterior): $100-200.
- **Power Roller** (for painting interiors): $50-100.
- **Cordless Drill** (for drilling work): $50-100.
- **Screw Gun** (for "hard to do" screwing): $30-100.
- **Circular Saw** (for all wood cutting): $50-200.
- **Nail Gun** (for nail driving): $150-400.
- **Heat Gun** (for striping paint and wallpapers): $100-200.
- **Sanders** (for sanding scratches on wood): $100-200.
- **Reciprocating Saw** (if the circular saw is not enough): $50-150.

Money Saver #4) Hire Students

Young people are willing to work for a lot less than an established contractor - in many cases young people will agree to work a full day for a payment of $50. You can hire students looking for work to do basic jobs such as weeding, cleaning, vacuuming or window washing.

Money Saver 5) Rent A Dumpster

Renovating is a "messy" job - you'll be left with a mountain of garbage once you're done and you must dispose of that. General Contractors apply extra charges for dumpsters which they rent and transport to a landfill. Many companies rent out dumpsters where the workers can dispose of garbage on a monthly fee. If you use the same dumpster rental company they can give you discounts being a loyal customer.

Chapter 7 - Completing the Flip

The Lowdown on Selling Your Property Yourself vs. Through a Realtor

You've made it - your $50,000 house is now worth $100,000! The money you invested in the house is now all reflected in the glitzy kitchen, the suburb bathrooms and updated interior. You've completed each step of the renovation and you're ready to sell the house and collect your paycheck. Should you give the average 6% commission (the equivalent of $6000) to realtors? Should you make a "for sale by owner" listing to save yourself to save that 6% on the realtor commissions? Decision, decision, decision!

What are the best ways to save money and sell a house? There are 2 main ways to sell a house: 1) Through a realtor and 2) On your own (for sale by owner - "FSBO"). If you choose a realtor you're giving them permission to take over the entire selling process: The staging, marketing and selling. You're also giving the realtor a cut at the end of the sale which is determined by a fixed percentage as high as 6% of the total sale price. Realtors are hired for more expensive homes on average. In 2008 a study conducted by the National Association of Realtors determined that the median price of a home sold by a realtor was $211,000 while the median of for-sale-by-owner listing was $153,000. Does this mean owners can't sell houses without a realtor? Definitely not! There are numerous ways to sell a house on your own and save thousands of dollars on a realtor. However, hiring a realtor carries numerous benefits in terms of efficiency and time – it's almost like hiring your own personal assistant.

The following are benefits of hiring a realtor that you never knew existed:

Realtor Advantage #1) Buyer's Realtors Won't Show FSBO Listings

Flipping Houses

Realtors who help buyers buy houses might refuse to show FSBO (for sale by owner) listings. This is because they know there's not going to be another realtor who can meet them and help them with the other end of the transaction. The buyer's agent might refuse to show your home to a buyer even if the buyer is trying to make them go for a visit.

The realtor will cite that dealing with FSBO listings is dangerous to their clients and that they shouldn't purchase houses without a representative for the seller. They want to get a guaranteed commission and they're weary of listings that don't have realtors shaking their hand on the other end. If you choose to sell the house on your own, you must be aware that other realtors will be put off by your house and know how to market to buyers directly.

Realtor Advantage #2) Realtors Are Emotionally-Detached

Selling the home can be an emotionally-draining because you've put months of work into the property - you will be tempted to get rid of the property at the first decent bid offer. Realtors know how to negotiate to get your the highest price for each house. When you hire a realtor, you're removed from the everyday emotional aspect of dealing with clients first-hand and this makes you less prone to making stupid decisions. "Stupid" decisions include overpricing the home, not countering low offers because you're offended by a low offer, or expediting the decision-making if you set deadlines for the selling. A realtor won't have the sense of desperation a flipper who's invested 6 months in the property will. If you sell the property you will likely nervously check your phone for signals (messages from buyers, inquiries, etc) and this can your judgment and affect your decision-making. Remove yourself from the process.

Rejection is a big negative too - if a realtor brings a client over and you show them the home, but they later decide they don't want to purchase the home the realtor will have to take that rejection. The realtor will only inform you once the property is sold and they won't tell you about individual meetings when they were rejected. It might be upsetting to hear some of the comments of potential buyers if you renovated the home yourself and this is why a neutral person such as a realtor can assist by keeping a cool head when showing the property to prospects.

Realtor Advantage #3) Selling Requires 24/7 Meetings

Selling house is a full-time job. Realtors work around the clock to show each individual property depending on when the buyers are available. What if someone calls you to see the home and you're stuck at work? You miss a potential lead. What if you're at a meeting and you get a buyer calling you with questions about the house? You can't be bothered with it. If you're working the whole day (especially on multiple properties), do you have the energy to explain to buyers each individual aspect of a home time and time again? Do you have marketing skills to show off each individual feature of the home? This is what a realtor does - they work around the clock selling properties and meeting clients individually. Your job is to purchase properties, renovate them and get paid. Realtors are invaluable when you're tied up between multiple properties and you don't have time to sell each individual property.

Realtors will give clients such as yourself a lockbox for the front door that allows them to show the home to buyers when you're away. Once all renovations have commenced, you'll no longer have a reason to stick around the property and the realtor can take over the sales procedure.

Realtor Disadvantage #1) Realtors Take A Big Cut

The only downside to hiring realtors is their commission. Should you hire a realtor? It depends on your priorities: If you want to save money above all, a 6% commission would sit better in your pocket. If you're financing multiple flips and don't have time to fiddle with each potential buyer, you should hire a realtor to take the weight off your back. We recommend selling yourself on the first flip because you'll keep more money and you'll learn the ins and outs of selling houses. If you hire a realtor right off the bat, you'll miss out on interacting with buyers and the lessons that ensue. The main reason to hire a realtor is to save yourself time: They do all the selling, prep work and dealing with prospects for you. If you're in the middle of 5 properties, you want a realtor to take over the sales process for you and allow you to focus on renovating properties. The opposite holds true: If you're new to the business, you can save thousands of dollars by NOT hiring a realtor.

Pro Tip: Be patient. If you've made successful renovations and priced the home appropriately, the offers will come in. You might not like certain offers and you may have to wait for weeks after you've started advertising the home to get a proper offer. Remain patient and price your home realistically, and you will likely get a fast sale (under a month!).

5 Best Marketing Strategies for Real Estate

You're ready to list the house and start getting offers. It's time to market your property aggressively - if you've chosen to forgo a realtor you'll be competing with hundreds of realtors in your area. You must schedule the placement of your house on the most popular real estate websites, upload the photos, communicate with buyers, schedule showings, and close the sale yourself. These are all things your realtor will do once you hire them, but you can join the process and contribute your own to make the sale go smoother. Marketing strategies can be applied even if you hire a realtor as they will essentially use the same marketing strategies - the only difference is that the property is more "prestige" if it's sold through a realtor and realtors meet buyers in person. There are many things you can do before you apply marketing such as hire photographers, write good descriptions, price the home adequately and filter the buyers.

Prep Step #1) Take Professional Photos

First impression matters not only for curb appeal when buyers arrive for a showing but online when they're browsing through hundreds of listings. You want your listing to stand out! To make that happen, you need to have professionals to take professional photos. Your iPhone photoshoot might get the job done, but a professional photographer will have a wide range of lenses and equipment that can enhance the colors of the property and make it look even better than it does in real life. Most photographers also have drones which can take aerial photos to showcase the surrounding neighborhood if it's in a great area. Aerial photos can expedite the sell a property by a margin of 30%. Most photographers are cheap and won't charge you more than a few hundred dollars for the shoot and post-processing. For the impact they can have on the sale of a property, professional photography a must-have.

Prep Step #2) Write Creative Descriptions

The first thing people notice once they open your listing is the description – they want to see if it captivates their attention. You don't just want to write "2 bedroom 2 bath going for $200,000". You want to write "2 bed 2 bath dream home, 5 minutes away from [City Attraction] going for only $200,000!". Take a look at dozens of properties and notice which descriptions stand out. Copy the writing style of those descriptions and replace them with your own information. If the ad captivated your attention, it will have the same effect on another prospect. Make sure to double-check for spelling mistakes and proofread your listings before you publish them.

Prep Step #3) Set Smart Prices

House pricing on the internet does not work the same as on real-life appraisals. When you meet an appraiser and/or compile your list of "comps" you will get a general value appraisal - this doesn't mean you should use that appraisal as the sale price of the home. What sells a home on the internet is "smart pricing". Instead of listing the home for

$200,000 it's much more effective to list it for $199,999. What impact will this have on the sale? On many websites people will narrow their search down based on price. If they search up to $200,000, they will be unable to see your listing. Smart pricing helps create a feeling of "affordability" because the property seems more affordable to the average person than the full price.

Prep Step #4) Filter Buyers

The main problem of online real estate websites is that they're open to all kinds of buyers: You might get interest from buyers who are not financially capable of purchasing a property. This is why realtors filter buyers in advance: The buyer's realtor checks their finances to make sure they're "qualified" and then they sends qualified leads to the seller's realtor based on the price range to make a quick sale. They in return get 3% each off the sale. The internet is the "wild west" in terms of prospects because you never know if they really mean business or they're wasting your time. Hiring a realtor who has connections to other realtors can help you save time by sending only qualified buyers at your location.

Top 5 Marketing Strategies For Real Estate

If you've successfully completed the creative work (photography, copywriting, pricing), it's time to make your property visible to future prospects. Even if your property is in top shape, you have the best pictures/aerial shots, you have good sales copy and pricing - no one will know your property exists unless you list it on big online websites. The following are the best ways to market a property on the internet (which are all free!):

Marketing Strategy #1) List On Real Estate Websites

To list your property online, start with the largest websites – the most prominent of which is Zillow. Zillow currently lists over 100 million properties for sale in the United States that include regular houses, condos, commercial buildings, foreclosures and more. Zillow can estimate the price of a property using similar listings and they have data for every zip code in the US. Their database is massive and they receive dozens of millions of visitors every day. A listing on Zillow will expose your property to thousands of potential buyers in your immediate area. The Zillow Group also owns Trulia.com which is a major player in the real estate industry. Currently listings on Zillow are free and they allow you to upload pictures, videos and key information about the property. Buyers will have access to your contact information and the ability to call/email you to pitch offers.

Marketing Strategy #2) List On Classified Ads Websites

The biggest classified websites on the internet are Craigslist and Nextdoor: Both of these are highly trafficked websites by people looking to purchase homes. Craigslist in particular is the largest classified ads website in the world and their listings are free, and you can re-create listings once your old listings expire. Craigslist will give you exposure to people in your area looking to purchase property and can make for a quick sale.

Marketing Strategy #3) Old-School Print Ads

Market the old-fashioned way - print out ads and plaster them in the immediate neighborhood. The people most interested in property in your area are going to be people who already reside there! Many times people are on the lookout for second investment homes that they can purchase and/or pass on to their children. If they're located right where they live, it's more convenient for them because they'll be able to stay in touch with family. You can print out a picture of your house, list basic details/sales price and plaster it all over the neighborhood such as local parks, bus stations, electric stands and more. You'll see ads like that all the time because this marketing strategy is still effective. If you want to take this a step further, hire a designer to make a brochure with your property that highlights the details of each room, and host "Open Days". Your realtor can help you organize open days that will last from the morning to the afternoon, typically on weekends. This leaves the home open for everyone who wants to check it out in person.

Marketing Strategy #4) Make A YouTube Video

You don't have to be Scorsese to make a "House Tour" for YouTube. To make a YouTube video, all you have to do is record a walk-around of the property: This will dramatically increase your interest online because people will have a feeling as if they're already in the house. It will also narrow down the list of people who are actually interested in buying the property because they won't be caught by surprise once they step foot on the property.

Many buyers dislike a home once they're at a showing because they don't know what to expect – they've only seen a few pictures. If a buyer sees a home tour and is still interest, this means they're more likely to purchase the property. Combine aerial videos that your photographer took with their drone and shoot a small 2-3 minute walk around of the property. When you upload the property, list the address and the city/zip code which will gather even more interest by people searching for that location.

Marketing Strategy #5) Create A Dedicated Website

The final step is to make a website for the property. Building a dedicated website might seem like a lot of work, but it's a worthwhile investment compared to simply listing the property on real estate websites. You can use plug-and-play hosting and site builder packages that enable you to create a website on the fly. Your special [yourdomain].com address will certainly be available and a package might cost as little as $10-20 a month. You only have to host a website until the property sells and then you can shut it down.

How to Stage Your Property to Win Over Buyers

Remember when you were a kid and your parents made you clean your room before relatives came over to make a good impression? It's time to put the finishing touches on your property and prepare it for showings – the property has to be in top shape and make buyers feel as if they're already living in it. This is called "staging". The final piece of the puzzle to selling a property is to stage the property for buyers. The realtor will organize "open days" where they pitch the property to multiple people and the interior and exterior have to be in top shape to make an impression. This means no debris from the saw dust your contractor left behind, no yellow patches on the lawn, no unpacked tiles waiting in the bathroom. The property has to be completely furnished, cleaned and ready to show-off. Realtors refer to the whole process as "staging". In many cases you want to stage a property before you start taking pictures and posting it online. Staging is not recommended for all homes: Most low-value flips don't require staging and realtors will skip open days in favor of a quick sale. Staging has to make the home feel as if people will live in it - the key to successful staging is to make it feel like a real home.

Buyers who attend open house days will pay attention to the cleanliness and maintenance level of the property. Two realtors will combine forces and bring over "qualified" buyers who are in the price range of the property, and buyers make impulsive decisions and purchase a property on a whim! This is why making a good first impression is imperative for the sale of the property. Even if you have to pay extra for power-washing and landscaping, it's worth it as it will expedite the sale of the home. The final decision buyers make will always be driven by emotion and if they perceive the house as high-value on arrival, they will be keen to buy it and place higher bids. This helps you because it takes your property off the market, saving you on carrying costs and allowing you to move on to the next property.

How Staging Works: The Basics

Staging works by highlighting the strengths of the house and camouflaging the weaknesses. Appearance is the sole driving factor behind 90% of all purchases in real estate, and the few people who are willing to buy a home that does not visually appeal to them are investors. Although no house is perfect, there are many features you can enhance in a typical house that will showcase the best parts of the house and conceal the worst ones. This usually comes down to smart decisions. **Example**: You have a large window that faces the sunset on the second floor. Don't make the mistake of covering that window and instead showcase it as a highlight. Add or remove furniture that enhances the size of the room.

Staging The Interior

To stage areas of the house such as the kitchen, you can either fully replace the outdated kitchen with a new turnkey kitchen (that can run up to $20,000) or you can simply replace appliances. A much faster way to stage a kitchen is to purchase new stainless steel appliances that will create a clean and crisp appearance for your buyers. The same applies for the living room: If you attach a shiny new plasma screen, this will give the living room an appearance of luxury and modernity.

Staging The Exterior

If the home has a large back yard with its own patio or deck area, don't leave it empty! Purchase a few solid chairs and a table in order to allow buyers to visualize their life and all the memories they could make in that back yard. The buyers have to picture themselves grilling there, playing with their kids and spending time with their family. To make that happen, purchase the furniture you need and facilitate these experiences. If the lawn is in bad shape, hire a landscaper who will spend a few hours fixing the "bald" spots on the grass and consider hiring painters who can paint the yellow grass green.

Staging Tip #1: Furniture Arrangement

Reconsider the furniture placement in the living room and bedrooms - buyers will analyze the space to sense whether they have enough space to comfortably move around the area. Arrangement is key here - make sure the sofas and chairs are placed in a way that enables conversation. If the room feels cluttered, dump the furniture in the trash. Many times you need a minimalistic design with the main sofa, a table and some side chairs. Focus on "conversational" alignment of furniture. Can the living room comfortably fit 5-10 people who are having a conversation? If the answer is no, purchase the furniture or re-arrange it in a way that enables conversation.

Staging Tip #2: Opening Up Space

Many small rooms such as the second room can feel cramped - to create an open feeling, move the furniture right next to the walls. This will open up the empty space and enlarge the space in the room. The opposite applies for large rooms - if there's too much space, pull the furniture towards the middle of the room which will free up space between the furniture and the walls. In both cases re-arranging can open up the space and show people that the rooms have space for movement.

Pro Tip: Furniture should indicate the way traffic in the rooms moves. Focus on creating fluid walking space where the person won't have to think about bouncing over pieces of furniture. Buyers should be able to navigate around large pieces of furniture such as beds and sofas.

Staging Tip #3: Buying Accessories

Invest in accessories such as flowers and books to enhance the sense of comfort in a room. If the rooms feel too "empty" you can purchase flowers and carefully place them on the tables or near the walls where they enhance the homely feeling of the property. Accessories should determine the purpose of a room. **Example**: The exterior should have relaxing rocking chairs where the residents can relax. The living room should have a main table and a place for books. Most accessories are inexpensive and universally-appealing, making the home more desirable for buyers.

Chapter 8 - Staying Smart

House-Flipping Mistakes to Avoid at All Costs

Think your $50,000 renovation budget couldn't flop? Even if you under-spend on your renovations, there are "red-flags" you should avoid before and after the purchase of a property. Details, details, details! When you're buying a house, when you're talking to contractors, buying insurance, sending inspectors and renovating you have to pay attention to the following "red flags" that could signal your property is going to flop in advance. The impact of failure under each one of these could reflect in tens of thousands of dollars lost on your bottom line. The two biggest problems you'll run into are acquisition price and contractor losses, and both will lay on your consciousness. The first problem is related to the purchase price: If you purchase a home for more than your initial budget, you will have less money for renovation which leaves you with little/no profits at the end. If you don't investigate your contractors and they do a sloppy job, you will have trouble selling the property at the end of each renovation.

1) Over/Under Renovating A Property

Example: If a property needs $30,000 in renovations: $10,000 for a bathroom, $10,000 for a kitchen and $10,000 spread over other miscellaneous costs - you shouldn't spend $50,000 (over-spending) or $15,000 (under-spending): You have to invest that exact amount! Focus on the upgrades the home desperately needs. Is the kitchen in good shape but the bathroom is falling apart? Spend 50% of your budget on the bathroom and spend less on the kitchen - it makes no sense to invest equally if one room is in worse shape than another. Things can get expensive fast: Something as simple as smart fridge can end up costing you thousands of dollars. Maybe skip working on the back yard and focus on the interior. Seek out lower cost tiles and floors. Buy cabinetry on sale. Buyers can't tell a difference between a

$5/sq ft. floor and $10/sq ft. floor - this could make a huge difference in your bottom line. Keep the renovations "easy" by focusing on the basics i.e. cosmetic repairs. The second you go into structural issues, roofing, foundation work - those are not "easy" fixes and your budget will be overblown fast.

Visit trade shows or "open houses" where you can see new suburban developments: What do they have on the inside? Check out their HVAC system, plumbing, electrical setup, kitchen appliances, etc. If investors are spending millions of dollars on developments they are making those bucks back big-time. This means their houses are trendy and you can copy directly for your property. To "wow" your future customers you should invest in small-time smart appliances such as thermostats, security systems and LED fixtures. This will solidify the value of your smart upgrades.

2) Taking Bigger Projects Than You Can Afford

If this is your first flip, start with small homes and never spend more than $40,000 on a renovation. Your magic number is $40,000 - this is enough to renovate most average homes in the United States. Spread that budget to $15,000 for bathrooms, $15,000 for the kitchen and $10,000 for minor purchases. If you start out with $100,000 renovations you will be overwhelmed by the sheer scope of the work and the management levels you'll have to put in at that level of rehab.

Progressively carry out bigger renovations to make bigger margins once you're fully aware of the risks involved and day-to-day dealings with contractors. Example: A large rehab might require tearing down a wall to open up the kitchen area to the living room. What happens when you tear down the wall? You have to purchase additional reinforcements, you discover molding, some termites can hide below the wall, and now you're paying for 5 other things at once (that you didn't calculate in your initial budget). All these issues can extend the time it takes to renovate and sell. If you focus on renovations under

$40,000<, you're putting yourself at minimal risk and you're almost guaranteed to sell.

Cosmetic repairs under $40,000 are "easy" and will familiarize you with repairs on all levels: You'll know how to carry out kitchen, bathroom and flooring repairs. You'll know how to fix the exterior and make the house have curb appeal. You'll know how to install security systems. This is when you'll be ready to move on to bigger upgrades such as changing the foundation, tearing down walls, joining rooms together, adding space/garages, and even adding/removing entire floors.

3) Forgetting To Network

The real-estate business is old-fashioned and people value "connections": You'll need a network of like-minded professionals who can help you flip your properties and act fast. What happens when you run into a sudden problem such as with bathroom tiles and you need a second sub-contractor? You could simply call your real-estate buddy and he will refer you to the adequate sub-contractors because he's ran into a similar problem before. The biggest pitfall before starting is not networking: Spend a month attending networking events and conferences before your first flip. Make friends in the business and visit their construction sites to offer them a hand. Once you have friendships you have people to rely on for advice and connections if you ever run into problems (which you will!).

4) Not Inspecting The House Before Purchase

The appraiser and realtor have to take a detailed look at the existing infrastructure to inform you of every upgrade you have to make - don't purchase a house before a detailed analysis. Many novice flippers are shy or over-confident and they think because a property is cosmetically in good shape that it's not going to require major upgrades. The appraiser has to take a detailed look at the HVAC system, plumbing, electrical, roof/structural shape, fireplace, and more to make sure the infrastructure of the home is on solid shape. Carefully evaluate the upgrades necessary because those will reflect in your renovation budget which has a direct impact on the net profit you're left at the end of each sale.

5) Overpaying For Houses

Let's say a home is worth $80,000 based on the appraisers/realtor's information but the seller asks for $90,000 - you should refuse to pay. Many novice flippers are driven by emotion and think because they ran into a good deal once, that they won't run into a good deal again. You tell yourself "So what, it's only $10,000!" but at the end of the day that money could have went in your pocket if you simply moved on. Remember that the purchase price can have a significant impact in the net profit you take home – the purchase price can affect this as much as the renovation cost. Calculate how much you can spend by estimating the ARV and the 70% rule and don't overbid a single cent. You should actually be down-bidding sellers the same way buyers will try to do once you sell your property. Remember the rule: Pay less, make more.

6) Forgetting To Increase Coverage Insurance

The second you renovate a home, immediately call your insurance provider and ask for additional coverage. Home insurance plans insure a home at 100% of the home value. What happens when you carry out renovations and the home value increases by 30%? You need an additional 30% coverage to cover up that spike. If you fail to increase the insurance and something happens to the home, you will lose significant money. As soon as you make renovations, you must rush to the insurance office to increase coverage on the home based on the new estimated value.

7) Not Screening Contractors

Think checking licenses and bonding is enough? No! You must thoroughly investigate each contractor as if you're stalking them: Call up their previous references, visit current construction sites they're working on, check their portfolio and visit those properties, read reviews on Angie's List and Google them to verify there aren't any horror-stories of investors dealing with those contractors. Once you've checked and verified their reliability, that's when you sign the contract. You can't trust a contractor with tens of thousands of dollars on blind faith. You want to make sure your investment is safe in their hands and the only way to do that is due-diligence research.

8) Hiring Overly Cheap Labor

What if you hire a cheap contractor and you discover badly placed cabinets in the kitchen with cigarette buds left all over the house? What if the contractor delays the work indefinitely but they take your money in advance? There are many things that can go wrong with cheap labor. Always opt for "average" contractors that have good reviews. The best contractors will over-charge you for basic work. The cheapest contractors tend to be unreliable (the work has to be re-done). Average contractors get the job done and they expect regular compensation. There are certain exceptions: If a lawyer is starting out at $20/hour you'll be suspicious because many lawyers charge 10x as much. However, if they want to build up their name they will be willing to work for next to nothing. Take advantage!

The aforementioned factors could affect your bottom-line by tens of thousands of dollars - be cautious! You can overspend at every milestone of the house-flipping business: Make sure each dollar you invest has a multiplying factor (for each dollar you invest you want to get at least two dollars back!).

4 Warning Signs Your House-Flip is Flopping

You're in the middle of a flip – what could go wrong that you can't plan in advance? If the windows won't open, if the door handle is jammed, if the paint-job feels off, there are many things that you will discover "in the moment" that you couldn't pre-meditate and you must fix right then and there. This is what we call "warning signs": Problems that pop-up mid-construction that you must calibrate for in the moment and solve them immediately. In most cases you notice warning signs when it's too late.

Example: A contractor finishes flooring and the floor is uneven. You then have to take out the uneven section or cover it up some way. You must learn from experience by making mistakes and fixing them. Most mistakes will not be your fault but the fault of the contractor. Even though 80% of all renovations go smoothly, the 20% can be a nightmare if you're on a tight budget and have to repeat a major job. Don't blame yourself because even an experienced contractor can mess up once in a while. Be cautious of the following warning signs during your renovation:

Warning Sign #1) Doors/Windows Won't Open

The biggest and most common renovation problem is a lack of careful placement of doors and windows. Many laborers will rush to "get the job done" and misalign the positioning or get the angles wrong. This way, you as the resident can't enjoy a casual walk through your home. **Example**: The handle on the door doesn't latch securely (loose bolts). The door doesn't close smoothly due to a bad angling. The door doesn't clutch property once it's locked but small pressure can open it. The same applies for windows: A small millimeter shift in windows can cause the house to not function as intended, and leak weather such as wind.

Many contractors only replace the door but forget to replace the jamb - this creates serious problems when the two are not aligned properly. To avert that, hire contractors who replace the jamb along with the door. This way everything aligns perfectly once you close the door. If you hire cheap labor you will experience a lot of sloppy work on details like these. The door and door frame have to square up for the job to be considered successful. Double-check to make sure the windows open and close properly. Test all the clutches. Contact the contractor and demand solutions if something goes wrong - you paid them.

Warning Sign #2) Bad Work In The Kitchen

Remember the phrase: "The kitchen is the heart of the home". The kitchen will sell your home and attention to detail in the kitchen is imperative. Your contractor must align the kitchen layout in a functional manner. If you have a bad layout in the kitchen, you can't camouflage that by purchasing shiny steel appliances and new granite countertops. The first thing you'll notice when you enter a badly-renovated kitchen is that the appliances aren't laid out correctly. There will also be gaps between the countertops and new doors that are badly installed on old cabinets. Good contractors will organize the "invisible" side of the kitchen as well. For example, under the kitchen sink you usually have the dishwasher connector, sink drains and garbage disposal at the same time. Make sure they don't interfere with each-others functioning and/or remove certain parts from there appropriately.

Warning Sign #3) The HVAC System Is Dirty

HVAC: Short for "Heating, Ventilating and Air Conditioning" is the temperature-management system of the house. The HVAC system is the key to any comfortable home. However, many times you can't see the debris that piles up in the house system during repairs which lasted for months. If the renovation lasted half a year, you have a lot of garbage to remove and must hire an adequate sanitation crew for the HVAC system. The HVAC is a nest for airborne bacteria and drywall dust. Put your finger on the blower fan blades and notice if they're full of drywall dust. If your finger is covered in the dust, this is a very bad sign. Take a look at the evaporator core of the air conditioner and get a professional crew to clean it at the end of renovation. This is going to be a cheap but significant renovation. Buyers might think the home is in top shape by looking at the cosmetic repairs you've made, but there are underlying repairs that you have to carry out for their own good which are invisible.

Warning Sign #4) The Flooring Is Uneven

There's no bigger warning sign than looking down and seeing uneven patches at the ground level - this is how you know your contractor screwed up! If you want to assess how fast your property will flip, take a look at the state of the flooring. If the flooring is butted up to base molding you must cut out the bottoms and remove the molding on the base. Once that's done, you can lay the flooring again.

In many cases mold will build up fast and you have to re-do the job. The flooring has to look right at the trim edges of the home because this is the first thing buyers will buy once they review the property. If the buyers notice poor flooring, this will be an indicator that the home was redone by clumsy contractors and they will assume the home has more serious problems such as electric work and plumbing that need to be fixed.

4 Exit Strategies to Always Keep in Mind

You put tens of thousands of dollars in a property, the renovations were carried out and it's about to sell. What happens if the house doesn't sell? What are the "last resort" strategies you can implement to prepare for a worst-case scenario? In house flipping, these are called "exit strategies". If a flip goes wrong, if everything falls apart, you must have an "exit strategy" to save your money and get out. Many FSBO listings fail due to a lack of marketing, no connections to realtors, bad renovations or all of the above. Focus on not overspending money on your renovations for a start. If your renovation budget is $40,000, don't over-spend by a cent. Try to lower your contractor expenses in advance, which ensures that if you do end up with surcharges you will afford it using the leftover cash. If you spend recklessly you will end up going over-budget on your renovation and this might delay your sale as you'll have to sell for higher than you initially calculated to break even. Most house-flips end up profitable and/or the flipper makes their money back in the least.

Pro Tip: Don't panic - You're safe. Once you've purchased a property you have an asset that you can re-sell even without renovating it. You can never fall too low unless you recklessly spend on upgrades that are not necessary.

Exit Strategy #1) Lower The Price

We don't like hearing it - the worst thing a realtor can say to a seller is "lower your price". However, this method is the fastest exit strategy to get out of a bad house flip. If the contractors messed up and you don't have time to re-do the jobs, simply lower the asking price and you'll probably sell the home in the first few weeks. If your property is worth $200,000 and your net profit is $20,000, it might be worth lowering that to $190,000 and only ending up with $10,000 profit rather than waiting for months to sell the property at the $200,000 price tag.

This way you can "get out" of a bad deal and move on to better properties with better contractors. Time is of the essence here, especially on borrowed money. Every day that your house sits on the market increases your cost and you'll be spending thousands in insurance premiums that probably spiked after you renovated the property. Lesser profits are a better option than staying on the market for half a year. Remember that your time is precious and once you get out you can take the lessons you learned from this property and apply them on the next one to make more profits. If you're reading this in advance, be cautious with your ARV estimates and nail your ARV up front to avert drastic exit strategies.

Lowering the price means accepting the loss and proceeding to do better. You will learn a lot by making lesser profits if your renovations failed due to bad contractors and/or side issues that you never expected. Even experienced flippers have issues that come up at the random. Accept the loss and make the next one a win! Remember that timing is important. If you spent only 3 months buying, renovating and selling you would be able to move on a lot faster. You're not emotionally attached to a property that you spent only a few months renovating. You will have at least 3 more tries to get this right in the same year. Whatever failed or went wrong that disallows you to sell the house at full ARV price, don't repeat that mistake again. You'll be smarter this time.

Exit Strategy #2) Offer A Lease

You have a motivated buyer looking to buy at full price - problem is, they can't afford a mortgage yet. The "lesser" is the seller (you) and the "lessee" is the person purchasing a property from you on an extended contract. They will be able to afford a mortgage 6 or 12 months down the line once they get a promotion, gather more money for a down payment, etc. In leasing, the buyer will be able to put down some deposit that you collect at the start of the lease. The deposit then secures their right to buy the property at an agreed date further down the line. This gives you some "get out" cash and security that you've found a buyer. You'll be able to feel some of the profits right away. Leasing implies that you both agree to certain "lease terms" - the buyer will be paying you a monthly leasing fee on top of the rent that will increase your cash flow and give them time to gather money for a full mortgage that will pay off the house and give you back your investment. Leasing is even smarter option than renting because the tenant has much higher interest in the property and agrees to purchase it at a fixed date. Their "investment" in the property means they'll take much better care of the property as they plan to live there forever. The initial down-payment/deposit on a lease should be at least 5 figures: $10,000-50,000 depending on the price of the house. This deposit is non-refundable.

It's legal to collect an "option down payment" which is the advance payment the lessee pays for living in the property. However, if they change their mind about the purchase of that property they will not be entitled to a refund. You will need a real estate attorney that can draft up the contracts that protect you against lessees who change their mind. This is a method employed by people who either expect to make more money in a certain time period that will allow them to buy the house outright, and it's used by people who already have access to capital but their credit rating is bad and they're not eligible for a mortgage. In many cases credit rating can be affected not only by reckless spending but simply a bankruptcy such as a divorce, death and/or health issues. There can be many scenarios why a person's credit was affected but they are still on the market to buy a home - you only have to give them the time to gather the money to fund a full purchase. You can charge them rent fees on top of the advance lease fee. This is the best exit strategy for people who don't want to lower their price on the sale but have time and want to solve the problem on a long-term basis.

Exit Strategy #3) Become A Landlord

The good old land-lord strategy is the go-to for people who don't want to settle for lesser prices and are heavily invested in a project. If your home value is $500,000 you probably don't want to let it go for $450,000 just to make a quick sale. In this event, the rent income you collect can cover your mortgage, utility bills, insurance, taxes and even leave you with some profits at the end to finance further deals. Rental income is serious business and many people specialize in buying cheap properties only to rent them out - not to sell. It's possible to rent the home and list it on the market at the same time, allowing you to collect income while you're trying to cash out on the big sale. If your loan has high interest rates the last thing you want is to default on that loan and get the property taken away from you after you've renovated it!

Pro Tip: It's much easier to rent a house than to sell it. You can find tenants for the house in as little as a week and once you sign a lease for 3 months or 6 months you can still show the property to potential buyers and tell them the move-in date if they're interested in purchasing. If you want to save money, rent out the home immediately and start marketing the home as a "for sale" home online. This way you will have a steady income that covers your carrying costs on top of offers from buyers. There is also a psychological side benefit: If buyers see people are already living in the home, they will associate this with a "finished" home and not something you renovated for a quick profit.

Research the local market. Is this an owner's market or a renter's market? Take a look at each individual house in the neighborhood and consult with the tenants to determine if they own those houses or if they're renting. Many markets are hot rental markets that you can take advantage of because people will always be looking to rent there. **Example**: If a property is located next to a Corporate HQ you will find many local workers who want to be in proximity of their job but don't want to buy a house yet. This opens up your property to a pool of potential renters who will find it easy to make payments and you'll collect rent each month.

This way if you're paying off your mortgage on a hard money loan or a private money loan, you'll be able to pay off the 8% interest rates easily until you sell the property at full price. Renting property is the way you can keep a property on the market without harming your pockets. If the mortgage, insurance and utility bills amount to $500-800 a month and you rent the property for $1500-2000 a month, you'll be left with $1000 in net profits at the end of each month. Unless you're on the clock and your deal was financed by a private lender who expects you to sell the house, banks won't care if you rent the house as long as they get their monthly payment.

Exit Strategy #4) Wholesale To Investors

The reverse of wholesaling a property at the starting point is to wholesale the property at the end point - many investors will be looking for new properties and you can wholesale the property to them to get out immediately. The new investor will pay off your initial investment and renovation value and they'll sell the property themselves. The main reason to wholesale a property instead of lease or rent out is if you're tied between multiple properties and you don't have time to deal with individual buyers/renters who you have to deal with every month. If you're financing 5 properties at the same time and one doesn't seem to go right, the best way to get out of it is to wholesale it to a different investor who is more motivated to take over this property. This way, you get your "get out" paycheck and the new investor gets a new property.

Conclusion – The Takeaways

We promise you this: Every morning you'll wake up excited. Once you've bought your first house and the renovations start, you'll wake up and rush to the construction site trying to get your hands dirty like you're about to move in there! House-flipping is an adrenaline-induced journey where you realize you're on the brink of making a huge profit and you're seeing your investments materialize in front of your own eyes. There are few feelings that can compare to a successful flip, once you've done all the work and put the finishing pieces together - you can do it.

We want to give you encouragement. You're in this for the long haul. If you start today, remember it might take you 3 months until you get to the first stages of flipping. That's the best case scenario. The average flip takes 6 months. Take your time and consider each step of the way carefully - and cross-reference the value points in this book every time once you run into trouble and need help. You'll forget most things we talked about, but as you gain experience you will internalize the lessons and flipping will become second nature.

We presented the nitty-gritty details you need to battle it out in the world of house-flipping. You now know how to pick properties, finance 6-figure deals, carry out renovations start-to-finish and finally market/sell houses to buyers. It's up to you to decide what to make of this information. You may act on this information today or postpone it and act 5 years from now when you're ready. The information will hold true then still - house-flipping has been around for decades and the same principle and methods apply.

In 6 Months You'll Be A Different Person

Take it slow - you're at the baby stages of house-flipping. You have a long way to go until your first "Sold!" sign. If you're nervous, it's normal because your life is about to change. One day you'll be calling realtors or property owners and buying your first home. 6 months from now you'll be shaking the hands of a new buyer who bought your home! You'll experience those initial "awkward" conversations when you try to convince sellers to give you a low price on their property. Maybe you'll dislike the sellers you're calling up or and maybe you won't like the properties once you step foot on them in person. Maybe the sellers will be great and you'll be eager to buy their properties. Congratulations – you've become a property owner!

You'll eventually have the pleasure of dealing with the "finance" people who will finance your whole flip: They'll provide the money for acquisition and bankroll the renovations. It's on you to estimate the repairs, run your calculations, decide the ARV, and spend that money adequately. You'll have to hire contractors and meet them in person: Scary business! You'll then watch people working for you and signing off their checks. Maybe you don't need contractors and want to get your hands dirty yourself? The buyers won't care if you did it yourself or hired a contractor as long as their property is renovated to their taste. Are you an experienced contractor who wants to get his foot in the flipping business? No one will be more competent at this job than you – once you finance the initial deals, you'll know how to manage a team of contractors under your wing.

Don't Waste Time - Start Now!

Even if you're only 12 months away from gathering the finances for your first down payment, time is invaluable. Make the first move and start visiting houses in your area "For Sale" and talking to realtors. Attend networking invents and meet like-minded people. Set the foundation and do the groundwork that would allow you the possibility of flipping houses in the first place. If you have little money to invest, work two jobs and gather the finances you need to put down the first down payment. Discover "deals" in your area and try to get in touch with investors who can finance those deals outright.

Start joining networking events, make connections on LinkedIn where you can communicate with real estate investors, attend construction sites and offer them a help in exchange for knowledge. You'll be surprised at how willing people are to help a young grasshopper. The more time you spend at the construction site, the more you'll be confident when it's your turn to flip. Offer value at each step: Pay people in cash for insider knowledge in your area. Offer free labor to an investor who needs help on his flip. They will share their knowledge with you and repay you once you start flipping and run into trouble.

Invent Your Own Method - Flip Your Own Way!

Finally, take the lessons you learned in this book and apply them your way: Invent your own method! It's important to determine how you like to get things done. Some flippers prefer short 3-month flips and make it their goal to flip a property in under 3 months. Others like to take a year and flip an expensive property for a large paycheck at the end of the year. The same principles apply to large-scale construction: Once you're familiar with house-flipping you can move on to bigger deals such as residential buildings and commercial buildings. Hiring contractors works on the same principle – it's only scaling up.

Maybe you like to furnish your properties with luxurious interiors. Make that your signature style of flipping. Maybe you only replace the basics and save money on every flip. Whichever "style" works for you can be replicated on multiple flips in the same year. Most flippers "go with the flow" and renovate each property on an individual basis. Everything could work in theory - find what works for you in practice. You could take over the whole process and carry out the renovations yourself. You could market the home yourself instead of hiring realtors. You could hire GC's and never actually set foot on the property. You could hire realtors and let them sell for you. All of those lead to the same result – a sold house. You'll be glad once your hand is graced with a 6-figure check and a "Sold!" sign – all that hard work will pay off in the end.

www.ingramcontent.com/pod-product-compliance
Lightning Source LLC
Chambersburg PA
CBHW031107080526
44587CB00011B/858